WHY VOTE LABOUR 2015

WHY VOTE 2015

LABOUR

EDITED BY
DAN JARVIS MP

WITH A FOREWORD BY
ED MILIBAND

\B^b\
Biteback Publishing

First published in Great Britain in 2014 by
Biteback Publishing Ltd
Westminster Tower
3 Albert Embankment
London SE1 7SP

ISBN 978-1-84954-734-5
10 9 8 7 6 5 4 3 2 1

A CIP catalogue record for this book is available from the British Library.

Set in Chaparral Pro

Printed and bound in Great Britain by
CPI Group (UK) Ltd, Croydon CR0 4YY

Contents

SECTION 3: A BETTER POLITICS

Foreword

ED MILIBAND,
LEADER OF THE LABOUR PARTY

Too many British families feel that the country doesn't work for them anymore. People are working harder but only just staying afloat, communities are fracturing, and parents fear for the future of their children.

These problems are not caused by any one political party, nor just by this government or the last. They were brewing for years before being exposed by the global financial crisis. And it will take more than the belated end of the recession to put them right.

Labour's mission is to build a Britain where hard work and talent gets its fair reward, where everyone gets a chance to succeed, and where the next generation can do better than the last.

Building that fairer, more dynamic and self-confident future requires big changes in the way our country is run. The Labour government I hope to lead in 2015 will change our economy so that every family – not just a wealthy few – get the chance to create and share in our country's success.

The next Labour government will build stronger public services with more childcare, better schools, and an NHS with the right values restored to its heart. And that government will change politics too so that it opens up to the people of Britain and ensures that every community in every region can play a full part in building a more prosperous country.

This book, *Why Vote Labour*, is a collection of essays from some of Labour's brightest thinkers which tell different stories about communities, values and ideas – but all united by a belief that a One Nation government can build that better future for Britain.

I would like to especially thank Dan Jarvis for organising and editing this book, and all the contributors for the time and care they have put into their writing.

I am immensely proud to lead a party with people like this who will help us build that future together.

Ed Miliband
August 2014

Introduction

DAN JARVIS MP

Why Vote Labour is a book about the future. It is about the future we choose for our country, about how Britain makes its way in the modern world, and the society we aspire to be in years to come.

At its heart is a simple premise: our country is on the wrong path and in desperate need of change.

There is so much that is right with Britain today. We have been through tough times over the past few years, but we are still a nation with a proud history and what should be a bright future. I find more reasons to believe that every week in my work as a shadow minister and a Member of Parliament. I meet remarkable young people with big dreams, talented entrepreneurs with fresh ideas, dedicated public servants working in world-class institutions like our National Health Service, and tolerant communities full of good neighbours looking out for one another.

My concern, however, is that they are all being let down by a government that is drifting at best and taking our country backwards at worst. You only have to look at what we have had to endure since David Cameron took office in 2010. Millions of families worse off and struggling to make ends meet, child poverty rising, record numbers of young people out of work, and a National Health Service pushed to breaking point.

As the general election draws near, I fear what Britain might look like after another five years of a Tory government looking to the past and complacently insisting we can carry on as we are when we should be working for success and building for the future.

This book argues that Britain can do better. Our country deserves better and, with the right leadership, we will do better. Britain needs a Labour government.

* * *

I am under no illusions in editing this book about the reality of our political landscape. I've knocked on enough doors in recent years to know that the key decision many people make on polling day won't be whether they vote Labour, Conservative or for any other political party. It will be whether they vote at all.

We face big, difficult national challenges, but the greatest obstacle we face is the increasingly widespread belief that our problems have outgrown our politics. Many people have completely lost faith in the idea that politics of any colour can make a positive difference to their lives.

The natural and fashionable temptation is to blame this loss of trust on sorry episodes like the parliamentary expenses scandal. This certainly caused a lot of damage. I should know – I was elected to replace an MP who was sent to prison for expenses fraud. I've seen the impact the scandal had on my community and felt how long it takes before trust begins to come back.

My personal feeling though is that this disenchantment goes much deeper. Many of the most disillusioned people I speak to have been shaken by global forces beyond their control. Too many feel cut-off by an economy that simply doesn't work for them, left behind from the rest of society and powerless to change their own lives.

Repairing these broken bonds of trust and restoring people's confidence in the power of the ballot box to change their lives will be the biggest challenge for my political generation. It is a task that asks big questions of our politics. It requires honesty and humility too.

This should start with the basic admission that politicians can't solve all our problems alone. We need to work to solve them together.

My firm belief in this is rooted in the life I had before I came into politics.

I served for fifteen years in the British Army before I was elected as the Labour MP for Barnsley Central in 2011. Some people still ask me how a major in the Parachute Regiment could possibly be a Labour supporter. The answer is that my service didn't conflict with my Labour values – it reinforced them.

I grew up in a home where both my parents went out to work every day to serve the public. My dad was a college lecturer, while my mum worked with offenders as a probation officer. The importance of community and the pride that comes from service were lessons that they and my wider family instilled in me from an early age. It was that belief in the value of service that took me into the armed forces and kept me there during some tough times.

I was commissioned from the Royal Military Academy Sandhurst in 1997, three months after Labour returned to government following a generation out of office. It was during another general election in 2005, as I listened to the results coming in over the radio from a bunk bed in the UK's military headquarters in Kabul, that I first began to think that life after the army could maybe include serving the public in a different way.

A by-election and several years later, my politics is driven by two things I learned during my time in the army.

The first is the potential of the individual – how people can overcome incredible odds and scale incredible heights. My service in the armed forces took me to Kosovo, Northern Ireland, Sierra Leone, Iraq and Afghanistan. It put me in difficult situations and tested me to my limit. Coming out the other side showed me that we can all achieve exceptional things when we have the right training, mentoring and support around us to help fulfil our potential.

The second is the value of the team. The most important thing to understand about the army is how close-knit a community it is. Your regiment or battalion brings together people from all backgrounds and with all manner of different beliefs. You live together, train together and, ultimately, you have to be ready to fight together. That relationship develops deep bonds of trust. You become accustomed to relying on others. You stick together. You do your bit, knowing that others will do theirs.

That is why I have always believed in the basic principle that we achieve more through shared endeavour than we can alone, and that we should work together to get difficult things done.

That essential spirit is why the Labour Party is my party. Much like the army in many ways, our party has a strong history and traditions, and has always been ready to respond to meet the challenge of changing times.

Labour has always been at its best when we have put our party at the service of the nation, reaching out to every class and community, bringing the country together, and creating a politics where everyone has a stake, plays a part and feels empowered.

Those are the values of Ed Miliband's Labour Party and the themes running through this book. It sets out a Labour vision for how Britain can succeed in a complex, competitive and changing world, and ideas for how we can build a society that makes the most of our talents and delivers equal opportunity for all, regardless of who you are or where you come from.

It is not a story I could possibly hope to tell on my own. That is why this book is also a shared effort, bringing together insights from shadow ministers, MPs, councillors, parliamentary candidates, trade unionists and other Labour supporters. It showcases the great team that Labour has ready for government in 2015 and our case is all the stronger for it.

What we have to say is not, and does not pretend to be, a manifesto or an official Labour Party mission statement. Neither does it seek to cover every commitment or policy area that will be up for debate at the general election. For one, much of the discussion on public services is focused on England, as the time of writing has coincided with the referendum on the fate of the United Kingdom and an ongoing debate about the future of devolution in Scotland, Wales and Northern Ireland.

What this book does aim to do is present a Labour view on the challenges facing our country, what our priorities will be and, ultimately, why you should place your faith and trust in us and vote Labour.

A small island in a changing world

The test for all parties going into the next election will be how to plot a new course for Britain in a stormy and rapidly changing world.

Global wealth and influence are moving from from north to south and west to east at an ever-quickening pace, information is everywhere, and we have never been more interconnected.

The middle class is expected to more than double to five billion people over the next two decades.[1] This global village has been brought ever closer together by an explosion in trade and financial connections. The number of goods bought and sold in the international marketplace has quadrupled in the last thirty years. A typical manufacturing company now uses parts and products from more than thirty-five contractors around the world – from Sweden to Taiwan and the USA.[2]

We've all become used to talking about how we compete with India and China, but now the debate is shifting to how Britain keeps up with fast emerging economies like Turkey, Mexico and Indonesia.

These forces of change are being further accelerated by technology. Many people now live their lives never out of reach of a smartphone with sixteen times the memory and 1,000 times the processing power

---

1   David Rohde, 'The Swelling Middle', Reuters, 2012.
2   Christine Lagarde, A New Multilateralism for the 21st Century: The Richard Dimbleby Lecture, February 2014.

of the computers that first took man to the moon. Innovation has packaged all of this into a device that is twenty-five times smaller and cheap enough for people around the world to carry around in their pocket.

Next year the world population is forecast to be outnumbered by mobile phones for the first time, with three quarters of the subscriptions in developing countries.[3] It's estimated that in the next five to ten years nearly every human being will have access to some form of computer technology.[4]

This technological revolution illustrates a wider trend that is unlocking new freedoms for people who have never had them before. Power is transferring from states to individuals.

This different future offers new potential and opportunity, but it also brings pressures and instability too, with new ills springing up as old ones are cured.

Take the changing face of enterprise. For much of the past century the left was focused on 'common ownership of the means of production, distribution and exchange' in industry.[5]

Today, anyone with a laptop, a broadband connection, a PayPal account and a 3D printer can start their own hi-tech manufacturing business.[6]

On the other hand, outsourcing to emerging economies and the replacement of human workers with computers through 'robo-sourcing' is moving jobs overseas and eroding the returns from well-paid work here at home.

Closer global connections also mean that other countries' problems can now very quickly become our problems too. Just ask my constituents in Barnsley whose lives were changed forever by the activities of bankers and property speculators in New York. Or

---

3   International Telecommunication Union, *The World in 2014: ICT Facts and Figures*, 2014.
4   Goldman Sachs Annual Report, 2013.
5   Original Clause IV of the Labour Party constitution before it was amended in 1995.
6   For a fuller explanation of this, see the RSA's Adam Lent, 'The Marxist revolution has begun but no-one's really noticed yet', March 2013.

think how stock market fluctuations on the other side of the world can hike up the price of a loaf of bread and how much it costs to fill up the car.

This lesson applies to our security as well as our economy. As well as on our own shores, the forces of change have also ratcheted up pressure on volatile states and fragile regimes. In an increasingly unstable world, the threat of terrorism and extremism now casts a far wider shadow.

At the same time, many of the most intractable problems that we've known and talked about for years are approaching crunch point. We're all getting older and living longer; the gulf between rich and poor is growing; our climate is changing; and there isn't much money around.

With all this in mind, it's easy to be pessimistic about our country's future. And this Tory-led government has given us plenty to be pessimistic about these past four years.

I believe we still have every reason to be optimistic. I say that because it is the moments throughout history when our country has faced its most daunting challenges that have led to our most enduring achievements. We can live up to this again, but only if Britain has a government that can respond with leadership based on the right values.

The right values for a better future

This is a time for Labour values. As the world continues to shift, Britain faces obstacles that will be hard to overcome and demand difficult decisions.

Now, more than ever, we need to be able to count on a government who will be on our side, protect us from dangers we cannot face alone and give us each the power to build a better life for ourselves and our loved ones.

We've experienced before what can happen when our leaders don't follow this path. When our economy was changing in the '80s the Thatcher government's response was to unshackle the market and leave everyone to fend for themselves in a game of 'survival of the fittest'. Communities in my constituency and across the country are still living with the consequences.

David Cameron used to talk as if he had learned from these mistakes. In times like these, 'we're all in this together' isn't actually a bad philosophy. The problem is that the Prime Minister's words have not been matched by his deeds. Any government that makes the choice to prioritise tax giveaways for the richest while inflicting the Bedroom Tax on the most vulnerable in our society cannot claim to be standing up for anything other than a privileged few.

Labour's values are different. They are written into the very constitution of our party – *to put power, wealth and opportunity into the hands of the many, not the few.*[7]

Our progressive politics has always been about spreading power and freedom in pursuit of a fairer and more socially just society.

We know that some people begin their lives better equipped than others to succeed in the future, whether by health, wealth or background. Labour strives to free people from these constraints.

It was the Labour Prime Minister Clement Attlee who once said that 'the aim of socialism is to give greater freedom to the individual.' It is a principle echoed by the Fabian socialist R. H. Tawney, an army veteran of the First World War, in his much-quoted 1944 essay 'We Mean Freedom':

> A society in which some groups can do much of what they please, while others can do little of what they ought, may have virtues of its own: but freedom is not one of them. It is free in so far, and only in so far, as all the elements composing it are able in fact, not merely in theory, to make the most of their powers, to grow to their full stature, to do what they

---

7   Labour Party Rule Book 2013, Clause IV, Aims and Values.

conceive to be their duty and – since liberty should not be too austere –
to have their fling when they feel like it.[8]

Tawney's aspiration for everyone to be able to 'have their fling when
they feel like it' may not have translated well through the years, but
the rest of his sentiment is timeless.

A genuinely free society is achieved not only through absolute
rights like freedom of speech and freedom of worship, but when
everyone has the opportunity to lead the lives to which they aspire
without being chained to forces that restrict people's life chances
like ill health, substandard education and poverty pay.

That has been the ambition at the heart of what Labour has
achieved every time the British people have trusted us to form a
majority government.

When Britain emerged from the Second World War in 1945, our
society was scarred by years of bitter conflict and being held captive
by Beveridge's 'Giant Evils' of want, idleness, ignorance, squalor and
disease. It was Attlee's Labour government that freed people through
a programme for full employment, a million new homes, the welfare
state and the creation of the National Health Service.

In 1964 Britain was changing socially and economically, and in
need of fresh leadership after a decade dominated by three aristo-
cratic Tory Prime Ministers. Labour and Harold Wilson responded
with a forward-looking government inspired by the 'white heat'
of technology that sought to free people from prejudice, taking
the first legislative action on race relations, equal pay and sexual
discrimination.

And in 1997 Britain was crying out for change. Our public services were creaking after a generation of neglect. Tony Blair took
office in a country where children were being taught in schools

---

8   R. H. Tawney, 'We Mean Freedom', a lecture delivered for the Fabian Society in 1944 and
     published in *What Labour Can Do* (London: The Labour Book Service, 1945), reprinted
     in *The Attack and Other Papers* (Freeport, NY: Books for Libraries Press, 1971), p. 84.

with outside toilets, patients were dying on hospital waiting lists and ministers viewed unemployment as a price worth paying for economic stability.

The last Labour government didn't get everything right, but the legacy we left behind is clear: two million new jobs, ten years of continuous growth, more than a million children and 800,000 pensioners lifted out of poverty,[9] rising living standards for all, an NHS with the shortest waiting lists and the highest levels of patient satisfaction in history, the first post-war government to cut crime (by more than 40 per cent), paternity rights and improved maternity rights, peace in Northern Ireland and the national minimum wage. All delivered with an average debt-to-GDP ratio lower than the previous Tory government, and the lowest proportion of national debt to GDP of any G7 country before the global financial crisis.[10]

Each Labour government has left the British people freer and more powerful than before. That is not something that can be said of the Tory government's record these past four years. In Cameron's Britain, powerlessness, inequality and insecurity have run riot.

At best, he has been shown to be complacent, neglectful and out of touch with the shared challenges our country faces. His policies have damaged the basic pillars of our society that we all rely on – from the NHS to Sure Start – and left many people feeling insecure and worse off in an economic cycle that doesn't work for them. It makes for a depressing vision of our country's future.

Labour remains ambitious that together we can build a more powerful Britain, one underpinned by the aspirations woven into this book – an economy that works for the many, an inclusive society and a better politics.

---

9 Department for Work & Pensions, Households below Average Income report, July 2014, p. 54 and p. 76.
10 OECD, 'Government debt', Economics: Key Tables from OECD, No. 21, 2014.

An economy for the many

David Cameron and George Osborne will ask you to decide how you vote by judging them on their economic record. Labour does not shrink from that debate, we welcome it.

However, much the Tories would like to rewrite history, the reality is that they have failed to keep their economic promises, failed to protect people's standard of living and failed to build the type of shared prosperity that Britain needs to succeed in the modern world.

When Labour left office in 2010, the economy was growing strongly, unemployment was falling and our country was on the road to a sustainable recovery from a financial crisis that had swept the Western world.

David Cameron's entry into Downing Street brought with it three years of stagnation and the slowest economic recovery in 100 years.

As Ed Balls points out in his opening to the economy section of this book, Britain is still expected to be borrowing £75 billion next year even though the Tories promised to eliminate the deficit by 2015. Having failed to achieve this in the past five years – despite having made it the centrepiece of their programme – why should anyone trust them to do it in the next five?

Cameron and Osborne also said they should be judged on protecting Britain's AAA credit rating, which has since been downgraded not once but twice.

And they ran on a manifesto pledging 'an economy where not just our standard of living, but everyone's quality of life, rises steadily and sustainably'.[11] In practice, their government is forecast to be the first since the '20s to leave people worse off at the end of the parliament than they were when they took office.

It is true that pressure on living standards has been growing for many years, not least due to the forces of globalisation. But when Britain has needed a government to respond to these forces, the

---

11   The Conservative Manifesto 2010, *An Invitation to Join the Government of Britain*, p. viii.

Tories have exacerbated them, pursuing an economic strategy based on lower wages, worse terms and conditions, and fewer rights for people at work.

The results are clear. Since 2010, job creation in low-paid sectors has increased at double the rate of the rest of the economy. We have seen a surge in zero-hour contracts, record numbers of people working part-time who want to work full-time, and the biggest fall in wages overseen by any government since the 1870s. For the first time ever, there are now more people living in poverty who are in work than in retirement or looking for work.

It all adds up to a recovery characterised by powerlessness. How can people feel empowered when doing the right thing and going out to work can still mean a life below the breadline? How can people feel in control of their own life if they don't know how many hours' work they will have from one week to the next? How can anyone feel free when they are forced to rely on vouchers for the local food bank because they cannot make ends meet?

If Britain is to successfully compete with new emerging powers with skilled populations several times greater than our own, then we need an economy that makes the most of our people's talents, not one that traps them on low wages and long hours. We are the country that unleashed the Industrial Revolution, made ourselves into the world's foremost trading nation and invented the internet. We can do better than going toe-to-toe with the sweatshop economies of the world in a race to the bottom that we would have no hope of winning.

Andrew Adonis, Chuka Umunna and Rachel Reeves each set out ideas in their chapters for how Labour can build an economy that delivers rewards for all, not just a few at the top. It is an approach built on four key elements.

The first is a simple commitment to ensure no one is left behind. Our economy is finally growing again, but this doesn't feel like a recovery for many people. We need to fix that so that everyone who contributes can feel the benefit of economic growth in his or her pocket.

The second element is championing enterprise, entrepreneurs and innovation. Our country needs more wealth-creators, not fewer. This is especially true in communities like mine in South Yorkshire, where we are still trying to replace the skilled jobs we lost during the '80s. It's only by backing business that we will deliver the growth, investment and good jobs we need.

The third element is fixing the underlying problems holding our economy back. Our economy is unbalanced, growth is too skewed towards London and particular sectors, productivity is too low, there aren't enough good opportunities for young people, and the link between growth and rising living standards is broken.

Drawing on the results of his growth review, 'Mending the Fractured Economy', Andrew outlines his key recommendations for how Labour can give our cities and regions the tools to become engines of prosperity, building on the urban renaissance since the '90s to make our towns and cities 'magnets for new and better jobs' and to spread wealth across the United Kingdom.

Chuka develops this theme further in his chapter, laying out how our reforms to support businesses and consumers will help restore the link between our national wealth and family finances. This includes building on what Britain does best through Agenda 2030 – Labour's plan to earn and grow our way to a higher standard of living – and tackling areas of market failure so that people can get a fair deal.

The fourth element is protecting dignity in work. Labour has always been the champion for ensuring people can make a better life for themselves through a hard day's work, whether through ending the scandal of jobs paying poverty salaries or granting better employment rights for part-time workers. I've played a small part in this myself in parliament this year by introducing my own Private Members Bill to strengthen the national Minimum Wage.

Modern life has placed new pressures on the workplace, but we won't achieve a higher standard of living in this century by sacrificing the hard-won rights that workers fought for in the last. Neither can we succeed if too many people who are able to work are unable to find work. Rachel takes on this theme in her chapter, outlining how Labour will value and reward contribution, tackle low pay through promoting a living wage, end exploitative forms of employment, and help more people into work through a Compulsory Jobs Guarantee.

These are the building blocks of Labour's economy for the many: better jobs, balanced growth, fairer markets, dignity in work, and opportunities wherever you live.

An inclusive society

Economic power is an important part, but only one part of how Labour will create a society of more powerful people. Satisfaction in life does not solely flow from the work we do or how much money we take home at the end of the month. It comes from the relationships we hold with one another, the time we spend with our kids, the enjoyment we get from sport and culture, being part of a community, love, stability, happiness, and feeling in charge of our own destinies.

Just as forces of change have challenged our economy, the twenty-first century has brought pressures that have entrenched powerlessness in too many aspects of our society.

Family life is under strain from falling living standards. Our stressful lives are increasingly haunted by spectres such as mental ill health. Our poorest communities are still the most blighted by crime. We can all expect to live longer, but for too many older people these will be years of loneliness and isolation. And all this against a backdrop of stubborn inequality and declining social mobility.

A society riven with insecurity and inequality is not one equipped for long-term success. We need an inclusive society where life chances are fairly distributed and no one is left out or written off.

We will only unlock our society's true potential when people feel empowered in their daily lives. I have asked Lucy Powell, Liz Kendall,

Bex Bailey, David Hanson and Polly Billington to discuss how Labour will seek to achieve this in four areas I think are of particular importance. Each of their chapters show how we will make a difference 'through big reform, not big spending', as described by Jon Cruddas in his contribution.

First, Lucy Powell discusses how we must begin by supporting the most basic unit of society: our families.

Labour is the natural party of family. We've always understood that families come in all shapes and sizes, and offered practical support in a non-judgemental way. The last Labour government alone introduced paternity leave, doubled maternity leave, guaranteed flexible hours for working parents, and created tax credits to specifically help families cover the cost of childcare. In contrast, by next year this Tory government will have taken away up to £15 billion in support for children in families.

Lucy sets out how the next Labour government will build on our proud record and take action to make life easier for mums and dads. This is important for two reasons.

The first is that, by 2015, Britain's families will have endured more than five years of falling living standards, with the cost of childcare and household essentials soaring while wages have stagnated. This has placed additional burdens on family life. Many of us will know families who have had to uproot loved ones and move home because of rocketing rents and insecure tenancies, or parents no longer able to read to their kids before bed because of the extra hours they're having to put in at work.

Secondly, we all benefit when families succeed and are collectively worse off when they don't. Our families are the best natural support system that many of us will have throughout our lives. When they break down it costs our society as much as £46 billion each year.[12]

I've seen in my work as shadow Justice Minister how young people

---

who don't enjoy a stable family life early on can be disadvantaged for
years to come. It underlines why Labour will prioritise prevention
and invest in early intervention to avoid the greater costs of failure.

This links to a wider point about the Tory government's unen-
lightened approach to slashing investment in services that many
families rely on. The reality is that closing more than 600 Sure Start
centres, reducing support in our children's early years, and cutting
back social community care is no saving at all when it risks storing
up much greater costs in the long run.

This is also true of the institution that takes us in when we are at
our most vulnerable – our National Health Service, which Liz Kendall covers in her chapter on how best to achieve longer, healthier
lives. Like most families, I have my own memories of when the
NHS was there for us.

My first wife Caroline was diagnosed with cancer in 2006. It was
a devastating blow, especially as our children were still tiny. Over
the next few years I experienced the best of what our National
Health Service can offer. I spent hours in hospital waiting rooms
and sitting with her through chemotherapy sessions. There were
also times when I couldn't be there as I was deployed in Afghanistan. Being away from home at that time was especially difficult.
Knowing she had the best doctors and nurses caring for her helped
keep me going.

Caroline died in 2010. Anyone who's suffered the grief of losing
a loved one knows how difficult it is to cope with the loss. At the
most difficult times you depend upon your family and friends, but
I will never forget how the NHS was there for us when we needed
it. Now is a time when we all need to be there for the NHS.

Sadly, it needs us more than ever. Over the past four years we've
seen it missing cancer care targets for the first time, leaving patients
having to wait more than two months for urgent treatment.[13] If

---

13   *The Independent*, 'NHS misses cancer targets for the first time ever', 30 May 2014.

we could lift our cancer survival rates to just the European average then we could save 10,000 lives across Britain every year.[14] But we won't reach this goal by carrying on as we are.

In 1997, Labour pledged to rescue the NHS, and we did. Liz's chapter sets out how we will do so again. Our plan will reverse the damaging effects of David Cameron's top-down reorganisation. And we will equip the NHS for the challenges of tomorrow, introducing an integrated model of physical, mental and social care that will empower patients by ensuring our doctors, carers and those who look after our mental health work much more closely together. Only a Labour government will ensure the NHS is still here for future generations.

Those future generations include talented and inspiring young women like Bex Bailey, who has written about the challenges she and her peers face in Britain today.

This is a tough time to be growing up. One of the most disheartening statistics about our country today came from the Prince's Trust earlier this year, which found that more than three-quarters of a million young people across the UK believe they have 'nothing to live for'.[15] It becomes more understandable in a context where many teenagers are leaving school facing high levels of youth unemployment, a housing ladder being pulled out of reach and a politics that doesn't relate to them. That's why I wanted a chapter specifically dedicated to how Labour will give our young people the best possible start in life.

I've spent much of my professional life working with young people and I've seen them do the most exceptional things. I don't buy the argument that the next generation is inferior in talent or energy to previous ones. They need a government that will help them fulfil their aspirations.

---

14   OECD 'Health at a Glance' report, 2013: http://www.oecd.org/els/health-systems/ Health-at-a-Glance-2013.pdf
15   The Prince's Trust Macquarie Youth Index 2014.

Bex uses her chapter to discuss how Labour will give young people better choices in our public life, including a bigger say in our democracy, a louder voice in our public services and an education that equips them with the skills to succeed in future careers that don't even exist yet.

The prospects for our young people is one of the subjects that people raise with me most often as a Member of Parliament. 'How is my granddaughter going to get a job?' 'Why aren't there enough places for my children at the local school?' 'How will they find a decent, affordable home?' With questions like these, it is understandable why these conversations often turn to what I know will be one of the most talked about issues of the next election.

Immigration is an issue Labour is ready to talk about, because it is a debate that needs our values. That is why I have asked David Hanson and Polly Billington to each draw on experience from their own respective communities in detailing how Labour will manage immigration in a smart, effective and progressive way.

Britain is greater because of the people who have come here through the centuries to make a better life for themselves – overseas entrepreneurs who have created one in every seven UK businesses, the doctors and nurses working in our NHS, and the Gurkhas I served alongside in uniform.

We won't create a stronger, more inclusive society by governments posturing and sending vans into communities with signs telling people to 'Go Home'. Labour will be guided by our values and by listening to people's concerns.

It is natural for people to be anxious about how our communities are changing when our economy and political system have left people in too many areas feeling powerless, left behind and struggling to get on in life. Labour will make it our mission to start to tackle this, giving everyone a fair and equal stake in our society, not left on the outside looking in.

A better politics

Building an economy for the many and an inclusive society will not be achieved by politics-as-usual. As the demands on our communities change, the response of government and how we do politics must change with them.

When Attlee's government sought to free people from the ills of post-war Britain seventy years ago, for instance, this meant the state taking direct action to give power to people who were out of work, without a home or without proper healthcare.

Labour still believes the state can be a force for good. Unlike the Tories, we are not blinkered by ideology into believing that less government always means better government. But the days when our problems can be solved by government alone are fading. There is no single lever that can be pulled behind a desk in Whitehall to solve the obesity crisis, find a cure for dementia or tackle climate change.

Neither can these issues be left entirely to the market. Competition can deliver progressive outcomes, but I don't want to live in a society where people are squeezed between market forces and an overbearing state. Our problems require a collective response that empowers the citizen over both.

To make this a reality, government today needs to be as much of an enabler, organiser and partner as a provider, manager or administrator. It needs to bring together the best of what the public, private and third sectors can contribute to meet each individual's needs. And if politicians want the people to put their trust in us, we must also learn to put our trust in them.

Harriet Harman describes in her contribution how a belief in 'the sharing of power for the greater good' is rooted in Labour politics. In their chapters, Stella Creasy, Steve Reed and Sir Steve Houghton each develop this theme, exploring how Labour can give people more of a say in the type of country they want to live in.

Stella reflects on political engagement and how Labour will take steps to create a stronger culture of participation and community involvement in public life. This can not only lead to greater empowerment, but also connect people with politics who otherwise wouldn't. Labour is well ahead of the other parties on this, but our commitment is to a politics that looks, feels and sounds more like the United Kingdom, with better representation for women, ethnic minorities and people with life experience outside of the Westminster bubble.

Steve Reed focuses on Labour's commitment to transforming public services, showing how communities can cut crime, get people into work and deliver better results when people are given more of a voice. This links closely to the Labour vision for localism in Sir Steve Houghton's chapter, who draws from his experience as leader of my own local Barnsley Council and as a member of Labour's Local Government Innovation Taskforce.

In contrast with the lack of substance behind David Cameron's failed promise of a 'Big Society', Labour's devolution agenda will break the mould of decades of centralisation and give communities real powers to tackle the issues on their doorstep. It goes beyond anything seen in England in the past 100 years.

Steve Reed and Steve Houghton both cite the successes of Labour councils across the country, highlighting two important lessons.

The first is a reminder that the best ideas can emerge locally. It was Barnsley Council, under Steve Houghton's leadership, that first pioneered what later became the Future Jobs Fund – a scheme launched during the final months of the Labour government which created more than 100,000 jobs, got young people back into work and saved the taxpayer money before it was wastefully scrapped by the Tories.[16]

The second lesson is underlined by the litany of examples in both chapters of Labour councils changing our communities for the better

---

16   Department for Work & Pensions, Impacts and Costs and Benefits of the Future Jobs Fund, November 2012.

– from Sunderland to Manchester and Greenwich. Today, Labour councils are leading the way in how to deliver progressive outcomes and better places to live on a tight budget, showing the difference that voting Labour can make across the country.

Bringing decision-making away from Westminster and closer to local people in this way will empower our communities, drive innovation and strengthen our politics.

A more localised approach however should not come at the expense of continuing our role as an open and outward-looking society on the international stage.

When the former Labour Cabinet minister Roy Jenkins wrote his own case for voting Labour before the 1959 general election, he made 'Britain and the World' his first chapter.[17] More than half a century later, the world has changed and has grown more complex, which is why I have chosen to end this book with a reflection from Douglas Alexander on the same theme.

More than a decade since I first served in Afghanistan, our country's deployment there is due to draw to an end. The world today remains dangerous and unstable, and much more interdependent, but ministers appear unsure as to what part Britain should play in it.

The clearest example of this was the government's 2010 Strategic Defence and Security Review – a rushed and deeply flawed exercise that will surely go down as one of the great missed opportunities of this parliament. Rather than plotting a new strategic course for Britain, the review acted as a crude cloak for cuts. The result was a confused conclusion that left our country with two new aircraft carriers but no planes to fly off them for nine years.

Four years on and the Tories still lack any vision for what our nation's role in the world should be. David Cameron doesn't have one, and in his weakest moments seems to be looking over his shoulder towards his Eurosceptic backbenchers to try and find one.

---

17   Roy Jenkins, *The Labour Case*, (Penguin, 1959) p. 13.

Douglas sets out how Labour will look beyond the horizon and deliver a foreign policy with progressive values as its compass, fit to protect our citizens and win the influence we need to succeed in the future.

A more powerful Britain

To be ready for that future, Britain must become a more powerful country. I do not mean powerful in the twentieth-century sense of the word, measured by the might of our arms or the size of our treasure. I mean a confident country made up of powerful people, each free from the forces that hold us back, able to go after their dreams and make the most of their potential.

This more powerful Britain is some distance away. How quickly we step towards it or whether we ever reach it at all will be shaped by how we respond to the challenges before us at the next election.

In a time of tough choices, immense challenges and rapid change, Labour is the party that will be on your side. When difficult decisions need to be made, we will always prioritise opportunity for the many over the few.

And we will be the party with ideas for an economy that works for the many, an inclusive society and a better politics. That's what this book is about.

SECTION 1

AN ECONOMY FOR THE MANY

'Are you better off than you were four years ago?' That was the question Ronald Reagan famously asked the American people in his first presidential election campaign. The answer back in 1980 was 'no' – and his Democrat opponent Jimmy Carter was thrown out of the White House after just one term of office.

Thirty-five years on, it's clear that Reagan's famous question will take centre-stage at the next general election. Every previous British Prime Minister in my lifetime has always been able to answer it by saying 'yes'. But David Cameron is currently set to buck that trend, with working people now £1,600 a year worse off on average since 2010.

And this failure to deliver rising living standards is not the only promise this Conservative-led government has broken. David Cameron and George Osborne famously said 'we're all in this together', but then gave millionaires a huge tax cut.

They said they'd balance the books by 2015, but borrowing is set to be £75 billion next year. And they said they'd rebalance the economy, but house building is at its lowest level since the '20s, business investment is lagging behind our competitors and our export growth since 2010 is sixth in the G7.

This failure presents a huge challenge for the next Labour government, but it is one we are determined to rise to with an economic plan to make Britain better off and fairer for the future.

As Rachel Reeves writes in her chapter, we will support working people, make work pay and tackle insecurity in the labour market. That means expanding free childcare for working parents, freezing energy bills, introducing a lower 10p starting rate of tax, increasing the minimum wage, ending the exploitative use of zero-hour contracts and giving tax breaks to firms that pay the living wage.

Second, we need to create more good jobs and ensure young people have the skills they need to succeed. So Labour will boost apprenticeships, transform vocational education and ensure there is a paid starter job for every young person out of work for over a year – a compulsory jobs guarantee funded by a tax on bank bonuses.

Third, we have got to build a stronger and more balanced economy. So a vital part of our plan is to get at least 200,000 new homes built a year and, as Andrew Adonis sets out, devolving more power and funding to city and county regions.

Fourth, we will promote long-term reform and competition in markets such as energy and banking so that they work better for consumers and businesses and support long-term investment too.

Fifth, as Chuka Umunna says, we will back British businesses by cutting business rates, maintaining the most competitive corporation tax in the G7, establishing a proper British investment bank and arguing for Britain to stay in a reformed European Union.

And finally, I am clear that the next Labour government will get the deficit down where this government has failed. We will balance the books and get the national debt falling as soon as possible in the next parliament. But we will do so in a fairer way, including by reversing David Cameron's tax cut for millionaires, tackling tax avoidance and cutting the winter fuel allowance for the richest pensioners.

There will be a clear choice at the next election: a choice between a Labour plan to make Britain better off and fairer for the future – with rising living standards for the many, not just a few – or more of the same from the same old Tories.

Ed Balls MP is Labour's shadow Chancellor.

Chapter 1

Mending the Fractured Economy: Better Jobs in Your Area

ANDREW ADONIS

Britain's industrial revolution changed the world. Innovation in technology, production and manufacturing transformed the lives of millions, first in Birmingham, Manchester, Leeds, and other towns and cities, and then beyond our borders, led by British exports. As well as output and population, wages saw unprecedented growth, with mass migration to new cities whose amenities and housing were improved by strong, civic governments.

Having once been the world's dynamo of new products, ideas and processes, British firms struggle to grow, find the skilled workers they require, and export. At long last, the UK economy is growing. But the economy is not creating the productive, high-skilled and well-paid jobs needed to raise living standards.

As business and civic leaders constantly told me during my year-long economic review for the Labour Party, deep structural problems need urgent attention: mass youth unemployment; skills shortages; too few high-growth companies which innovate and export; poor infrastructure; and excessive centralisation in Whitehall.

My report, *Mending the Fractured Economy*, sets out a plan for a new economy which spreads prosperity and restores the link between growth and living standards. Ed Miliband has already endorsed the key principles of this vision. The imperative is not just more jobs, but better jobs; not just more companies, but strong-growth companies which innovate and export.

Government needs to become smarter and more entrepreneurial, nationally and locally. Working in intense collaboration with leaders across education, business, science and public services, it needs to facilitate innovation, promoting higher rates of business and export growth. It needs to mobilise the huge, underexploited resources of state-funded research and development and government purchasing, as well as England's schools and further and higher education systems. We also need a new generation of strong, far-sighted city and civic leaders, with bold, credible plans for the amenities and infrastructure their localities need, working in close partnership with business and social leaders to make their towns and cities magnets of new and better jobs.

This is Labour's mission for our country.

Big strengths, big weaknesses

Big strengths and weaknesses characterise the UK's economy. Britain is home to some of the world's leading universities and some of the most productive researchers in the world. There are many successful companies and we have an open economy that is one of the leading recipients of inward investment, something which is closely tied to our membership of the European Union. Yet growth is unbalanced. The link between growth and living standards has been broken, exports are weak, young people widely lack the opportunities they deserve and inequality is vast, both between people and between regions.

The facts are stark. Nearly one in five under 25-year-olds is out of work or training.[18] Investment, including in research and development, is far lower than for our main competitors.[19] Productivity, which is the main determinant of our future living standards, remains a fifth lower than the G7 average.[20] We have barely a third as many young apprentices as the Germans;[21] our infrastructure is rated twenty-eighth globally by the World Economic Forum;[22] and the UK's balance of payments deficit recently hit the worst level for fifty years.[23]

The reaction of the Tories to my report illustrated why they are going so wrong. They tried to claim that there was no problem with regional inequality when this not only flew in the face of the facts, but also jarred with the experiences of millions of people living inside and outside London.

Having met with hundreds of business, civic and social leaders to hear the challenges their local economies face, I have been struck by the extremes of optimism and pessimism that hold sway. Optimism at our capacity to succeed, and the brilliant success of places like Cambridge with its high tech and bioscience, Warwick and Sheffield with their advanced manufacturing, Manchester with its advanced materials, Oxfordshire with its Formula 1, and the surge of innovation and energy from Tech City and Canary Wharf in London. But intense pessimism exists too about unskilled young people, about isolated businesses without the support they need to invest and export, and about towns and cities with creaking infrastructure and no plans for the future.

---

18 Office for National Statistics (2014), Labour Market Statistics.
19 OECD (2014), Main Science and Technology Indicators.
20 Office for National Statistics, International Comparisons of Productivity – Final Estimates.
21 International Labour Organization (2012), Overview of Apprenticeship Systems and Issues.
22 World Economic Forum (2014), Global Competitiveness Report 2013–14.
23 Office for National Statistics (2014), Balance of payments quarterly first release – current account.

Better jobs in your area

To create better jobs nationwide, Britain needs more strong-growth companies which innovate and export. High-growth companies are critical to creating new and well-paid jobs. Just 6 per cent of high-growth businesses generated half of the new jobs created by existing businesses between 2002 and 2008.[24] And these companies had one important factor in common: they were highly innovative.

Most innovation takes place in clusters, as firms in specific industries locate close to one another to benefit from a deeper pool of skilled talent, proximity to firms offering support services, and a flow of ideas between firms and other institutions such as universities. Many of these clusters exist in city regions, which have increasingly become engines of growth, creating the vast majority of new jobs.

Although London is a pre-eminent global city and has become an innovation powerhouse, England's larger cities beyond London have not been so successful, with only one, Bristol, generating above national average GDP per capita.[25] The cities and regions outside of London and the south east have industrial clusters but these are not strong enough.

Cambridge, a city of only 125,000 people, is pre-eminent among England's innovation clusters. Over 1,500 science- and technology-based companies, employing 54,000 people and with total revenues of more than £12 billion a year, are based in and interact in the city and its hinterland. Cambridge University and the consultancies and research institutes spawned by the university over decades have been critical to this success. Cambridge has also benefitted from sharply rising national science budgets after 1998, and from an influx of overseas students, researchers and professors. The success of Cambridge is a model for others.

---

24 Nesta (2009), 'The vital 6 per cent: How high-growth innovative businesses create prosperity and jobs'.

25 Rt Hon Greg Clark MP & Greg Clark (2014), *Nations and the Wealth of Cities*, Figure 5, p. 37.

However, Cambridge also illustrates the growth challenge. Inadequate transport infrastructure, a serious housing crisis and technician-level skills shortages are holding Cambridge back. These typify a wider national problem, which requires leadership and powers at regional level to overcome.

Anna Turley, Labour's prospective parliamentary candidate for Redcar:

'Redcar, a town built on steel-making and manufacturing, has been fighting for many years against a prevailing view that saw post-industrial decline in areas like ours as inevitable. Thanks to the hard work of local people, and particularly Community Union members, our mothballed steelworks is now back up and running and about to turn a profit.

There should be a bright future for industry on Teesside, but we need a strong, active industrial policy that will enable areas like ours to drive the British economy, just as it did in the past. We need to grow the skills of our young people so they can win the new jobs of the future, invest in our infrastructure and support for our fantastic industrial and manufacturing supply chains.

The frustration is that there is no doubt about the economic, social and natural resources that exist in so many parts of our country currently lagging behind London. Our region has a trade surplus above the national average, faster growth in exports, world-class universities and we are leading the way globally in advanced manufacturing, chemicals, pharmaceuticals, automotives and offshore wind. The North East could be the engine for British economic revival. It needs a government that believes in us and is ready to support all our regions.'

A smarter state

Government needs to radically rethink the way it interacts with businesses at both national and local levels in order to create the best environment for firms to grow. The state can no longer spend its way out of difficulty, so it must be smarter.

On skills, the UK has extremely high levels of youth unemployment and chronic skill shortages. Too many young people are poorly educated and essentially unskilled. Yet even among those with some skills and qualifications, there is a serious mismatch between the skills on offer and the demand for technician-level competency, particularly for roles requiring science, technology, engineering and maths (STEM) skills. And fewer than one in ten employers recruit apprentices[26] compared to a quarter of employers in Germany.[27]

As Bex Bailey also discusses in her chapter, the imperative is for a major expansion of high-quality vocational and technical education and STEM apprenticeships for young people, offering more and better work-and-train opportunities in all sectors of the economy. Local Enterprise Partnerships (LEPs) – as the regional voice of business leaders – should be responsible for driving the take-up of apprenticeships with local employers and ensuring that skills providers offer courses that lead to employment.

Links between schools and employers need to be radically strengthened, and I have recommended that a Director of Enterprise and Employment should be appointed to every secondary school responsible for promoting apprenticeships and work experience, and ensuring students receive better employment and careers advice. There also need to be far stronger pathways for technical education. More young people should be encouraged to study the maths and science subjects required for STEM careers, with a recruitment drive for specialist STEM teachers with significant experience in business and industry led by a new 'Teach Next' organisation. And I have proposed that at least 100 University Technical Colleges should

---

26   UKCES, UK Commission's Employer Perspectives Survey 2012, December 2012.

27   Data for 2008, cited in: National Audit Office (2012), Department for Business, Innovation and Skills; Skills Funding Agency: National Apprenticeship Service: Adult Apprenticeships: Appendices Two to Four, p. 3.

be established around the country by 2020, focused on developing skills for growth areas of the economy.

On innovation and science policy, we are lagging behind our competitors in terms of our ability to exploit our world-leading scientific research base. There should be another ten-year science strategy, repeating the successful model of the last Labour government, and there should also be a ten-year innovation strategy. In both cases, funding should be agreed at the outset for at least a parliament, and they should be priorities for investment. We also need more applied innovation centres, which bring together scientists and businesses to commercialise research on the model of the successful German 'Fraunhofer Institutes'. Britain has only seven 'Catapult Centres' compared to sixty-six Fraunhofers in Germany.

Small firms also need far better access to government procurement and research contracts. Chuka Umunna discusses in his chapter how Labour would champion this through a new Small Business Administration. The US experience has shown this is crucial to scaling up early stage companies. Government departments have significant research and development budgets – including £1 billion per year for health – but more needs to be done to mobilise these budgets and drive innovation.

The Small Business Research Initiative (SBRI), which is modelled on a similar US scheme, supports small businesses to drive innovation in public services, but its impact has been limited. While the US awards around 4,000 contracts a year on average, worth $2.5 billion, over the last four years the UK has launched just 124 SBRI competitions, averaging £25 million per year.[28] The government should also practise what it preaches and contract to a far greater degree with small- and medium-sized businesses.

Whereas the US has a requirement that small businesses receive at least 23 per cent of all federal contracts, in Britain they receive just

---

28   Technology Strategy Board (2013), Delivery Plan Financial Year 2013–14, p. 5.

10.5 per cent of government contracts.[29] I have recommended that the proportion of government procurement with small- and medium-sized businesses should be increased to 25 per cent of prime contracts directly with government and 25 per cent indirectly through the supply chain, with a new, more transparent target for contracts in the supply chain.

On infrastructure, Britain continues to underperform. According to the Civil Engineering Contractors Association, the 'infrastructure deficit' between the UK and our competitors is costing the UK around £78 billion per year in lost output.[30] At a national level, we need an independent National Infrastructure Commission, as recommended by Sir John Armitt and announced by Ed Miliband, to set out national infrastructure requirements for the next twenty-five to thirty years, and a government prepared to act on its recommendations, including in sensitive areas such as airport expansion and new power stations. A decade of inaction on runway capacity in the south east is inexcusable, and our country is facing a crunch in our energy supply in the coming years.

Sir John Armitt, former chairman of the Olympic Delivery Authority and author of an independent infrastructure review for Labour's Policy Review:

'Growth is good. It creates change, opportunity, jobs and a better life for all. It is dependent, in part, on good infrastructure fit for the future. New infrastructure can be expensive and too often is subject to short-term policies. We need long-term plans based on sound evidence and cross-party support.

That is why I have proposed an Independent Infrastructure Commission. It would produce a thirty-year assessment of our infrastructure

---

29   Cabinet Office, 'Making government business more accessible to SMEs: Two Years On', July 2013, table p. 4 and http://www.sba.gov/content/small-business-goaling (accessed 06/06/14).
30   Civil Engineering Contractors Association (2013), 'Securing our economy: The case for infrastructure'.

needs, to be passed to the Chancellor who would lay it before Parliament for approval. Secretaries of State would bring sector infrastructure plans to Parliament with specific projects to meet these plans over the coming decade. These plans would be debated and approved, with the whole process repeated every ten years.

Some people have interpreted my proposal as taking the politics out of infrastructure. Not so. Infrastructure is best delivered with cross-party support and consistent political leadership. That is the long-term approach that Labour has committed to.'

Mary Creagh MP, shadow Secretary of State for Transport:

'Many parts of our country are being held back from achieving their full potential by creaking transport infrastructure, limited connectivity and the rising cost of getting to work.

The Tories have failed on transport infrastructure, ducking the big decisions on airport expansion, cutting roads budgets then restoring them, and presiding over the West Coast franchise fiasco, which cost taxpayers £50 million.

A One Nation Labour government will focus on infrastructure to support jobs and growth, transport integration to drive efficiency and give communities greater powers over their bus and rail services.

With transport costs rising, greater local accountability is all the more important. Transport is now the second largest expenditure for UK households, after housing costs. Bus fares are up but passenger numbers are down outside London. David Cameron has failed to stand up for working people, allowing train companies to hit passengers with inflation-busting fare rises. Regulated fares are now 20 per cent higher on average than in 2010. Labour will ban train companies from hiking fares above a tough cap and give passengers a legal right to the lowest fare.'

Strong cities and regions

We also need to create strong city and county regions across England, with powers and budgets handed down from Whitehall to tackle infrastructure and skills weaknesses in particular. The establishment of the Mayor of London and the Greater London Authority has been one of the best pro-growth reforms of the last fifteen years. The new London government has overhauled buses and trains, transforming services for the better, tackled congestion, and constructively supported business through the development and planning process. The Mayor of London should get more responsibility – and England's other great city regions need institutions to match. During my tour of England's regional cities for the review, I found far more people who could name the Mayor of London – and his predecessor – than the leader of their own local authority. England's provincial cities need a new generation of Joseph Chamberlains, and the sooner the better.

'Combined Authorities' should be encouraged, whereby local authorities across city and county regions combine for common strategic purposes, similar to the role of the Mayor of London. Independent LEPs should be reformed and strengthened to give businesses a direct say over policy priorities, particularly local infrastructure. The existing thirty-nine LEPs, which were hastily set up to replace the Regional Development Agencies, require significant improvement. LEPs need to be rationalised where they do not reflect the geography of city and county regional economies, and form strong relationships with a coterminous partnership of local authorities.

In return, government should grant LEPs five-year capacity funding for their running costs, including research to underpin economic strategies, and ensure LEPs have the right of sign off on local growth strategies and investment plans for economic development, housing, transport and adult skills.

The level of funding devolved to city and county regions should be tripled to at least £6 billion per year to allow them to shape local provision of skills training, employment schemes, infrastructure and business support. And the full revenue from Business Rates should be devolved to Combined Authorities so that any additional income can fund infrastructure priorities and incentivise investment to drive growth. These proposals are far bolder than anything the government has delivered and also far bolder than anything Lord Heseltine proposed last year in his independent growth report for the coalition. Heseltine ignored tax devolution, despite the fact that city and county regions in the UK keep just 5 per cent of the tax revenue raised in their areas,[31] as George Osborne would not have supported devolution. For all the Chancellor's rhetoric about 'northern powerhouses', he has refused to give northern cities any power.

My report also highlighted the need for a step change in the way that government helps firms to expand and export. There needs to be significantly more support for financing new growth businesses outside of London and the south east, with the state investing alongside private investors. One of the government's schemes to help support growth firms via 'business angel' investments has invested just a third outside of the south east and the east of England.[32]

Labour has committed to supporting a network of regional banks alongside a British Investment Bank. We should also learn from the US, where Small Business Investment Companies (SBICs) have invested around $20 billion of long-term capital in firms via debt and equity investments from 287 SBICs around the country. This investment has helped to fund companies such as Apple, Sun, HP and Intel in the early stages of their development.

UK Trade and Investment (UKTI) and UK Export Finance (UKEF), Britain's export promotion and credit guarantee agencies, also need to be far more ambitious in supporting companies, particularly in emerging markets. UKEF provided guarantees for around ninety

---

31   Core Cities (2013), 'Competitive Cities, Prosperous People: A Core Cities Prospectus for Growth'.
32   National Audit Office (2013), Improving access to finance for small and medium-sized enterprises, Figure 15, p. 38.

companies supporting just over £2 billion of exports in 2012, compared to €42 billion in Germany and almost €8 billion in Belgium.[33]

While big numbers dominate discussions about economic growth, the real story exists in the company, or the cluster, or the school, or the city. All my proposals on innovation, skills, infrastructure and devolution seek to help them in practical ways.

They are designed to ensure that everybody in every region gets the chance to create and share in Britain's future prosperity.

Labour promises transformation for every part of our country, reviving our great cities and regions so that no one is left isolated and everyone gets their chance. Together, we will build on the best of Britain – the spirit of the industrial revolution – and we are optimistic that the best is yet to come.

Andrew Adonis is a Labour peer and shadow Minister for Infrastructure.

---

33   Note, the UK data excludes a one-off deal for a fighter jet which skews the underlying trend. British Exporters Association (2013), 'UK Export Finance: Supporting the National Export Challenge', p. 13 (authors' calculations for exchange rates).

Chapter 2

An Economy for All

CHUKA UMUNNA MP

'The future is still so much bigger than the past.'

— Sir Tim Berners-Lee, inventor of the world wide web

When I meet my constituents – on Streatham High Road, in my surgeries and on the doorstep – what they say they want is a job that is secure, with pay they can live on; a place they can call their home, in a strong community; good local schools; careers for their children, with a bright future; support to turn a good idea into a viable business; and help getting new skills for new jobs.

My constituents are full of ambition. But they do not ask for the earth. They are quite modest in their expectations of the help they will receive. All they are asking for is the chance to get on. They want a supportive community giving them a place to stand. They want a solid foundation on which they can build a future. They want some protection from forces of change that are beyond their control. They want to be able to believe that tomorrow will be better than today.

The problem is that even these expectations, modest for a country as rich and powerful as ours, can feel a long way off. Too many of my constituents are being let down by an economy that is no longer working for them. They might hear about the new opportunities in the global economy and from technological change, but what they see and feel is insecurity. Like people all across the UK, they have seen their pay fall while the cost of living rises. After four years of Tory-led government, wages after inflation are on average £1,600 a year lower than in 2010.

They feel the insecurity of an economy where rights at work have been cut and zero-hour contract jobs proliferate, with analysis showing that there are now 1.4 million zero-hour contracts. They see one in five young people who are unemployed, and nearly half of recent graduates doing jobs that do not require a degree.

More broadly, they understand the vulnerabilities of an economy where growth is unbalanced by sector and region, business investment remains low, and export performance is poor. These problems began before the recession and they will not be solved by its belated end. Growth might be a step in the right direction, but so many more steps are needed if our economy is to deliver for young and old, north and south, east and west, and over the long term.

The specific task for the next Labour government is clear: to build an economy of shared prosperity, ready to succeed in a world of change. It is to offer a real future to all my constituents, whatever their starting point, whatever their aspirations and whatever route they choose. It is to open up the vast opportunities of the global economy to all, while offering protection from the risks of a changing world that no individual or community can manage alone. It is to restore the broken link between a growing economy and rising living standards for all. This is an issue of fairness, but it also the key to the sustainable and resilient economy we need to thrive as a nation.

A society that respects the dignity of labour is a good society, and an economy generating well-paid jobs is an economy set up to succeed. Labour places central importance not only on employment, but also on increasing the numbers in self-employment, freelancing, and running micro businesses. Such an economy will be able to sustain higher wages because it is more productive. It will be an entrepreneurial economy, succeeding in export markets because it is making more goods and services that people want to buy. It will be a more resilient economy because it will be built on a broader industrial base and sustained by the taxes of more people in work.

Higher living standards for all are partly a function of the distribution of the wealth that is created, but also of the underlying productivity of the economy. These two factors come together in the quality of jobs our economy is creating. Among OECD nations, the UK has among the highest incidence of low-paid jobs, at more than a fifth of our workforce, while the middle of our labour market has become hollowed out. Under the last Labour government, the UK made substantial progress closing the productivity gap with our main competitors, but since the financial crisis this progress has gone into reverse. Output per worker remains 6 per cent below its peak.

This is significant. HSBC predict that UK GDP will grow 0.35 percentage points a year slower, on average, than growth for all developed countries up to 2030. Over the same period, they predict Germany will grow, on average, 0.65 percentage points per year faster than the UK. These differences are small year to year, but compounded over the next decade and a half they mean that living standards in the UK will have fallen by 5 per cent relative to the average of developed nations, and by 10 per cent compared with Germany.

Changing this trajectory and ensuring that rising productivity is translated into higher living standards for all are not things that can be achieved easily with a few quick initiatives. The productivity gap with other competitor nations is longstanding. The historic link between rising productivity and rising wages was broken before the financial crisis hit. It will take more than a recovery to fix it. To build an economy that works for all will require deep long-term changes, within a tough fiscal environment: big reform, not big spending.

The investment horizons for business stretch well into the next decade. To unlock that investment, governments should have the same long-term focus. That is why Labour has set out Agenda 2030, our long-term plan to earn and grow our way to a higher standard of living for all. It is a plan to build a high-productivity, high-skilled, innovation-led economy. It is a vision of a better-balanced, more resilient economy succeeding in the world, creating good jobs and opportunities, offering people a ladder up and the chance to make the most of their potential. It is bold, ambitious and the only way we can secure the future the British people deserve.

To get there will require three fundamental changes in approach to the way our economy is structured and run. The first is extending opportunity by investing in all of our people, providing a firm foundation on which people can build, creating pathways to long-term success through a career or through enterprise. The second is in reducing concentrations of power within our economy which undermine performance, reduce fairness and limit opportunity. The third is a relentless focus on productivity, not limited to markets and exchange, but including the processes by which value in our economy is created, along with the strategic leadership and institutions needed to support this.

Real opportunity

Extending real opportunity is the defining mission of our party. In today's world it is also an economic necessity. In a world of global competition, we cannot afford to waste the talents of anyone or to restrict the pool from which ideas can come.

So first, we must invest in the talents of all, not just those choosing university and an academic path. Bex Bailey rightly identifies in her chapter the need for quality training and support for the 50 per cent of young people who do not go to university. That is why the next Labour government will introduce a new gold standard for apprenticeships and increase the number of high-quality apprenticeships for young people through a something-for-something deal with employers – giving them more control over apprenticeship standards and funding, and in return asking that they create more high-quality apprenticeships in their sectors and supply chains.

Second, just as we need a national mission to train the next generation of apprentices, so we must provide a platform for success for entrepreneurs from every background. Britain's future success depends on businesses of all sizes succeeding, but every oak tree was once an acorn. There are many motivations people have for starting a business, and not everyone aspires to world domination. Every business wants to succeed on its own terms. We need this diversity to create broad-based, vibrant local and regional economies.

That is why Labour will offer real, practical help to those running small businesses – on business rates, energy costs, access to finance, business support, and late payment. We need a tax and benefits system, and regulations, suitable for the increasing numbers of freelancers or otherwise self-employed.

Under this government, business rates for small firms have risen by £1,500 on average. A Labour government will cut and then freeze business rates for 1.5 million small business properties, saving them on average over £400 over two years, paid for by not going ahead with the government's planned cut in corporation tax in 2015.

Helen Hayes, businesswoman with seventeen years' experience and Labour's prospective parliamentary candidate for Dulwich and West Norwood:

'Our small businesses provide thousands of jobs and demonstrate the enormous talent and creativity our country has to offer. That includes an exceptionally diverse range of businesses in my community, from traders in Brixton market to our factories in West Norwood. Many of them have had to lay off staff or close altogether over the last four years, however.

Having set up my business at the age of twenty-three, I know what makes business tick. We started ours in a former warehouse where we could rent individual desk spaces and increase or reduce our space

> with one month's notice. Affordable, flexible space like this is vital for
> start-ups. We need to protect it in the face of rising property values.
> Labour's approach will give businesses across the whole country the
> confidence to commit to growth.'

Energy costs are also a real burden for many small firms. Labour
would freeze energy prices until 2017, saving small businesses over
£5,000. Once the price freeze is in place, Labour will reform the broken energy market to ensure a fairer deal for business and household
customers. In addition, Labour will prevent energy companies from
rolling small businesses over onto more expensive tariffs without
their consent, insist on fair repayment terms for small businesses
that fall behind, and limit backbilling to a year.

The challenges for small firms getting access to finance are longstanding but have been exacerbated by the financial crisis. There is
insufficient competition, with four banks controlling 85 per cent
of small business lending. Banks should be fighting for the custom of
small businesses, not the other way around. Working through the
Competition and Markets Authority, Labour will ensure that there is
greater competition, with at least two new sizable challenger banks
and restrictions on the market share any one bank can have.

We need more competition within banking, but we also need more
competition to banking from alternative sources of finance like fac-
toring and peer-to-peer lending. Government too must play its part
in addressing the persistent structural problems small firms have
faced in accessing suitable finance. Labour will establish an independent British investment bank and a network of local and regional
banks with responsibility to increase access to finance for small businesses in their area.

Labour will also establish a new Small Business Administration,
based on the successful example from the USA, to make the whole
system work better for small businesses. This will put the voice

of small business at the heart of decision-making. It will focus on working to see that small firms get access to at least a quarter of government procurement contracts, and support excellence in local provision of business support services. It will take action to address the scandal of late payment, where small firms are effectively bankrolling larger firms they supply to the tune of around £36 billion.

Victoria Groulef, small business owner and Labour's prospective parliamentary candidate for Reading West:

'Reading is jam-packed with small businesses: hairdressers, consultants, builders, child-minders and caterers. Like me, they run their own small businesses. They need policies to enable them to get on, employ more people and contribute to the economy.

It's not easy for small businesses at the moment. One shop owner told me she pays almost the same on business rates as on rent. She calls it the cost of doing business, and her costs keep on rising. Labour's plans to freeze business rates would make a huge difference.

Another business owner I know is desperate to expand her business. She needs to take on a couple of employees. She is client- and skills-rich, with a packed work schedule and an impressive business plan. The banks will not lend money to enable her to grow. A British investment bank, offering advice and making local lending decisions, could unlock her potential.'

An economy that works for all must be built by all so that prosperity can be shared by all. We do not believe that it is only a few people at the top who create wealth, so Labour will invest in the talents of all of our young people, generating the skills that can support business to pursue higher value competitive strategies.

We know there is an exciting future within our grasp, a new era in which everyone has the chance to make and share in prosperity,

so Labour will create a more entrepreneurial economy, where the
practical barriers facing budding business owners and insurgents
breaking into new markets are swept aside.

This is an agenda to help Britain and business succeed together.
We are resolutely pro-business in our approach and also determined
not to offer just business-as-usual.

Power in your hands

A central insight of Labour's approach to the economy is the damage
that concentrations of power can inflict. They inhibit the function-
ing of markets, the performance of companies, the effectiveness of
decision-making in business and government, and the fairness of outcomes. This weakens our society, but also puts limits on our nation's
economic success. Our nation's economic strength will come from
democratising power, not concentrating it in the hands of a few. An
economy where power is better balanced will become a more resilient economy.

It is why Labour places such importance on the effective func-
tioning of markets. Competitive markets reward creativity and new
ideas, increase productivity and drive higher standards of service.
They provide the discipline at home that can drive success abroad.
Markets work best when environmental and social costs are included
in the price, not borne elsewhere. Markets work best when all parties are on a broadly equal footing, and have genuine alternatives.
They are less efficient when one side of the deal is dominant in power
or information, or when choice is limited. Low barriers to entry allow
new entrants to challenge existing players and keep them on their
toes. In this way, vigorous competition is good for consumers and
good for British business.

Labour will be unapologetic in promoting competitive markets in
the public interest. This relates to questions about how individual
markets are structured and designed, but also to dynamic questions

about maintaining a healthy distribution of power. In the minority of cases where there is evidence that markets – like energy and banking – are broken, Labour will act to fix them, in the interests of all.

Caroline Flint MP, shadow Secretary of State for Energy and Climate Change:

'When the gas and electricity businesses were privatised in the '80s, the Conservative government promised a competitive market that would deliver a better deal for consumers, competitive prices and sustained investment. Over twenty-five years later, it is acutely clear that privatisation has failed to deliver on this promise. Gas and electricity prices are uncompetitive. Bills are rising year on year. The market has failed to unlock the investment the country needs. Public trust and consent has been lost.

A One Nation Labour government will reset this market to ensure we deliver on the original promise of privatisation. We will create a genuinely competitive market that works for Britain's families and Britain's businesses. Government will take greater responsibility for enabling the investment that will guarantee our energy for generations to come and keep us on track to decarbonise our economy. And in the time it takes to implement these changes we will protect consumers from any more unfair price rises by freezing energy bills until 2017.

Britain deserves better than a government that stands up for a privileged few and an economy that doesn't work for millions of working people. That's why this plan is part of One Nation Labour's plan to build a different type of economy. One where the British people feel the country is run for them, in their interest and for their future.'

Second, just as concentrations of power can reduce the efficiency of markets, so the concentration of political power can be equally damaging. As Andrew Adonis, Steve Reed and Sir Steve Houghton set out in their chapters of this book, Labour will decentralise and devolve real power and resources from Whitehall to our cities and regions. Andrew Adonis' report to the Labour Party suggests that more than £30 billion of funding could be devolved to Combined Authorities, existing local authorities and LEPs over the course of a parliament – three times more than is planned now. This would include funding for housing, skills, transport and business support services. Where cities and regions are able to make a real difference to local growth, they will be able to keep and invest the higher business rate yields in things that will support future growth, creating a virtuous cycle.

Third, concentrations of power within organisations can reduce accountability, worsen company performance and create unfairness. We can see this in the spiralling of executive pay, quite detached from company performance. The groupthink that may result from taking account of only a narrow range of opinions and interests can mean market opportunities are missed.

Labour will promote policies that result in greater transparency, accountability and responsibility in corporate pay, and encourage decision-making that takes account of a broader spectrum of views, including the voices of employees. Labour will require boardroom remuneration – along with high pay outside it – to be transparent and clear. Labour will require employee representation on remuneration committees. Across the economy, Labour will encourage greater pluralism in ownership structures, including more mutuals and other forms of employee ownership.

We also need to tackle low pay and rebuild the link between the success of the economy as a whole and the finances of ordinary working families. As well as building an economy that creates more well-paying jobs, this includes ensuring that people are better paid for the work they already do. Rachel Reeves will discuss our plans for this further in the next chapter, such as encouraging firms to pay a living wage. Labour will not mandate a living wage, but we understand the clear benefits to employers and employees, to society, and to the public finances of encouraging businesses to pay a living wage where they can afford to do so.

In markets, in public decision-making, within firms and in wage-setting, Labour sees the economic as well as social imperative of encouraging productive and fair relationships. Sometimes this means central government doing more to promote competition, as in the case of the energy and banking markets. Sometimes central government is part of the problem, and the solution lies in decentralising power so that decisions are made by those closer to the action. Sometimes this means setting a fair framework that encourages dialogue and a reasoned approach to decision-making.

Supporting productivity growth

Closing the productivity gap and ensuring a fairer distribution of the wealth that is created are the keys to raising living standards for all. Investing in the skills of all and supporting entrepreneurs will help with both goals. So will changing the distribution of power in our economy, supporting growth in every part of the country, and making markets work more efficiently in the interests of everyone. These two shifts in approach also need to be complemented by a third: we must do more to boost productivity.

The aim is to support firms to take a longer-term, broader view of the value they create, and then make the investments needed to get there. This means changing the rules of the game to support long-term decision-making. It means strategic leadership from government to give firms certainty about the direction of the economy and to unlock investment. It means developing the institutions that permit collaboration outside of the market on issues like skills and new technologies, even as firms compete fiercely in the market.

So, to support firms taking a longer-term approach, Labour will abolish rules on quarterly performance. The bias in the tax system towards debt finance can create short-term vulnerabilities for firms, so we are considering the case for introducing a new tax allowance to encourage equity finance. Labour will also support a more long-term and rational approach to takeovers by limiting the voting rights of shareholders who buy into the company after the takeover has been announced and looking to extend the public interest test to support the UK science base.

Labour believes that government must play its part in enabling business to invest for the long term by setting clear strategic direction. We have committed to keeping corporation tax rates at the lowest in the G7. But we will also build on the sectoral strategies pursued by the last government and this, with an ambitious, cross-government industrial strategy. As well as an independent Infrastructure Commission to address the UK's long-term infrastructure needs, Labour will establish an independent Energy Security Board to ensure we have the energy capacity we need.

To develop the high-value jobs of the future, we need to be at the forefront of innovation. For example, the opportunities of transitioning to a lower carbon economy are vast. To ensure it is an opportunity to be grasped not a burden to bear, firms need certainty over the destination and real support to help them get there. That is why Labour will back the 2030 decarbonisation target, and give the Green Investment Bank borrowing powers so that it can support the development of new, low-carbon technologies.

Will Straw, Labour's parliamentary candidate for Rossendale and Darwen:
'The need to cut carbon and upgrade our energy system presents a major chance to take back our energy system and create future jobs. We urgently need to better insulate our homes, reduce dependence on polluting fuels from Russia and the Middle East, and replace ageing power stations. Over £200 billion must be spent on this over the next decade but only half this investment is forthcoming, mainly from state-backed companies in countries such as France, China and Scandinavia.

To avoid a security crunch, we need a target to virtually eliminate carbon pollution from our power sector by the end of the next decade. There is also a massive opportunity for citizens and communities to invest. Cities like Manchester are already taking a role with local generation, energy efficiency and fuel poverty programmes.

We need to power up this agenda and Labour is the only party committed to doing it – giving investors certainty by setting a target to clean up our power supply by 2030 and giving the Green Investment Bank proper powers to invest.'

Labour will ensure a secure and long-term framework for science and innovation, and seek to develop the role of institutions largely conceived or established by the last Labour government, like the Technology Strategy Board and the network of Catapult Centres that support growth and innovation. Developing these institutions is the final part of our approach to raising productivity. The absence of institutions that enable firms to compete effectively on issues like technology development and skills have long been a feature of our particular version of capitalism and something which has put our businesses at a competitive disadvantage.

By putting control of apprenticeship funding in the hands of employers together, Labour will foster the development of employer-led organisations to support this needed cooperation on other issues of common concern too. Linked to the development of the role of universities in their regional economies and giving employer-led LEPs real influence over spending in their region, this will begin to address a longstanding gap in our economic institutions.

Labour's plans to build more houses will also have a direct impact on the productivity of the construction industry and its supply chain. Ed Miliband has pledged that under Labour there will be 200,000 homes being built a year by 2020. Councils will be given a 'right to grow' so that they can release the land for new homes. Developers who hoard land to increase its value will be forced to allow homes to be built.

Emma Reynolds MP, shadow Housing Minister:

'Labour wants the next generation to achieve their dream of owning a home and ensure everyone has a decent, stable, affordable home. Too many are finding that dream is slipping out of reach, or find themselves renting privately in accommodation that is insecure, expensive and substandard. If you've just joined a waiting list for a social home, there are 1.6 million families already in the queue.

The Tories are presiding over the lowest level of house-building since the '20s. They've failed to stand up for 'generation rent'.

Labour will restore the dream of home ownership and reform the private rented sector. We will double house-building from where we are today. Labour will tackle the instability of our private rented sector to give security and peace of mind. Labour will ban letting fees for tenants and we will introduce longer-term tenancies of up to three years with predictable rents.'

Conclusion: an economy for all

Labour's historic mission has been to lift people up so that they can meet their aspirations. Today, this mission requires us to build an economy that works for all, connecting everyone to the vast opportunities of the fast-changing global economy.

So why vote Labour? Vote Labour for a Britain where you and your family can have confidence about our nation's future prosperity and your future within it. Vote Labour for a Britain where you and your children have the opportunities and support to meet your aspirations. Vote Labour for a fairer Britain with a level playing field, tackling unhealthy concentrations of power that limit opportunity, damage economic performance and generate inequality. Vote Labour for a Britain where investment is supported, entrepreneurs are encouraged, and we remain at the forefront of innovation. Vote Labour for a higher-productivity economy creating more well-paying jobs in every region of our country – jobs offering direction, purpose and a future. Vote Labour for a Britain where your work is valued and respected and your voice is heard. Vote Labour for a future in which business and Britain succeed together.

Chuka Umunna is the Member of Parliament for Streatham and shadow Secretary of State for Business, Innovation and Skills.

Chapter 3

A Britain That Works

RACHEL REEVES MP

'Work is about more than making a living, as vital as that is. It's fundamental to human dignity, to our sense of self-worth as useful, independent, free people.'

— Bill Clinton

The party of work

The Labour Party was founded on a belief in the value and dignity of work. As Ed Miliband has reminded us, 'the clue is in the name'.

Ours is a party born of the self-respect and solidarity of working-class communities, forged in the early struggles for the right to work against a background of mass unemployment, and for the eradication of the exploitation in the first factories and sweatshops.

In the '40s, the Labour Party, under the leadership of Clement Attlee, first committed the government to securing full employment, alongside the system of social security for working people proposed by William Beveridge in his report, which famously had people queuing around the block to buy it.

Since then it has been the Labour Party that has delivered historic advances in health and safety at work, the Equal Pay Act, and, under the last Labour government, the national minimum wage. I was recently reminded by a constituent of mine that before then you could still walk into a jobcentre and see adverts that read: 'Security guard wanted – £1 an hour, 100 hours a week. Supply your own dog.'

The Labour Party has always stood for the millions of men and women who go out every day to try to earn a living for themselves and their families. And today the right and responsibility to work, and the need to recognise and reward effort and contribution, is central to our mission of building a One Nation economy and society where everyone gets the chance to create and share in a new era of prosperity.

Of course there will always be some people who can't work, temporarily or permanently – because of sickness or disability, or the need to care for children or other family members. These people contribute to our country in many other ways and deserve our respect and a decent standard of living.

But for almost everyone, paid work is a major part of our everyday lives, and our life story. The work we do is a big part of who we are. It is how we provide for ourselves and our families. It is often where we find our friends and form our relationships. It is where we learn, develop our talents, do our bit and make our mark. That is why most of us aspire to find work that is not only fairly paid, but also fulfilling and rewarding.

The Tories are the party of long-term unemployment and a low-wage economy. Successive Conservative governments have lacked the philosophical basis, or the political will, to take the bold action to tackle the worklessness and low pay which blights lives and costs our country so much.

This is why the Conservatives opposed the introduction of the national minimum wage, and why they are relaxed today about the rising numbers on low pay, the prevalence of exploitative zero-hour contracts, the failure of most people's wages to keep pace with the cost of living and the spreading sense of insecurity about the future.

This attitude is bad for those who need a government that is on

their side. It is bad for our economy and our ability to earn our way
out of the cost-of-living crisis – because we can't prosper over the
long term if we are not making the most of everyone's potential, and
we can't keep the costs to taxpayers of our social security system
under control if we are not making sure that as many people as possible are in work and earning enough to make ends meet.

That is why a central part of Labour's mission for Britain is to get
more people into work, to make sure work pays, and to make sure
our system of social security and pensions provision recognises and
rewards the contributions people make over their working lives.

More people in work

Under the Conservative-led government we have seen youth and
long-term unemployment soar to record levels. Headline unemployment figures are now at last coming down but far too much damage
has been done to people's lives and life chances. There are still too
many people who risk being left behind – from young people with
low-skill levels to older workers who have found themselves redundant, as well as disabled people who want to work but are not getting
the support they need, and parents who can't get the childcare they
need to balance work and family life.

This isn't just a lost opportunity for those affected, it is a cost
to the country as a whole. Experience shows that someone who
has spent over a year unemployed when young is likely to have
lower earnings and further periods of unemployment later in life.
The Association of Chief Executives and Voluntary Organisations'
(ACEVO) commission on youth employment estimated the average
cost to the Treasury in lost tax revenues and extra benefit pay-
outs for a young person who spends a year unemployed is £2,000
a year. Our country is all the poorer if we are missing out on the
contributions of people who want to play their part but find the
system stacked against them.

The government's answer to long-term unemployment was the 'Work Programme', which was supposed to provide jobseekers with the advice, support, training and work experience they need to get back into work. The latest figures show that after two years on the Work Programme, which only becomes available after a year on benefits, more people have been sent back to the jobcentre in the same position as they started – unemployed – than have found a job through the programme.

A Labour government would take tough early measures to prevent a spell out of work and living on benefits from turning into months and years on end.

A key part of this is making sure people are equipped with the skills they need to succeed. At a college recently I met a young man training to be a decorator who had never had his dyslexia diagnosed at school. He was learning to read for the first time so he could check the details on the paint tins. He knew that being able to read and write would help him to get and hold down a job. Most of all, he was proud that he could now read the newspaper he used to take to work 'just to look the part'.

Labour will reward young people who sign up for training – not encourage them to sign on for benefits without giving them the support they need to find work, knowing that without support they are likely to spend a lifetime drifting in and out of low-paid, low-skilled jobs. Young people aged eighteen to twenty-one without the qualifications needed to get a decent job would not be allowed to sign on for Jobseeker's Allowance, but would instead be expected to continue in training or further education, with financial support available to those whose parents are on low-to-middle incomes as is now provided for young people at university.

With our Basic Skills Test, anyone signing on for Jobseeker's Allowance would be assessed for basic maths, English and IT skills within six weeks of their claim, and required to do any training needed to fill any gaps.

We would also build on the last Labour government's progress with developing effective welfare-to-work policies, replacing the Work Programme with a back-to-work regime that works. We would commission back-to-work support closer to the ground, so it will be better tailored to suit local economic conditions, and give a bigger role to smaller and more specialist charities and social enterprises who know what it takes to tackle the barriers some people face to getting into work.

To provide a backstop that means no one can remain out of work and on benefits for years on end, as happens today. Our Compulsory Jobs Guarantee will ensure that anyone out of work for two years, or one year for those aged under twenty-five, will be placed in a proper job paying at least the minimum wage for six months, alongside continued training and job search activities aimed at getting them a permanent position when the placement ends. This will be funded by a tax on excessive bank bonuses and limits to the tax relief that people with incomes over £150,000 can claim for their pension contributions.

Those receiving benefits and help to find work, or benefiting from the Jobs Guarantee, will be expected to accept their responsibilities – fulfilling requirements to train or accept a job placement. Those who don't will face losing their benefits. Our approach will be tough but fair – making sure unemployed people do what they need to do to get into work, but also making sure they have the proper support and opportunities they need to do so.

A Labour government will also do more to help those who want to work but face particular barriers. Older workers who have been made redundant or find that their skills are not up to date with the needs of the modern job market will be offered more tailored and specialised advice at jobcentres. Labour will make sure that disabled people are properly and fairly assessed and, if fit for work, given the right support to find suitable and sustainable positions.

As Lucy Powell writes in her chapter, parents of young children who want to work will be helped by our extension of free childcare for working parents of three- and four-year-olds. This could help 135,000 parents who want to get back to work or increase their hours to go out and do so – which will also boost our tax revenues. Labour will also make sure all parents with children at primary school can access 'wraparound' care from 8 a.m. to 6 p.m. to fit around their working day.

Tackling youth and long-term unemployment, and raising employment rates for groups who are particularly disadvantaged, is critical in building a Britain that works, and an economy that enables everyone to play their part.

While work for all who can is essential, it isn't sufficient. We need to make sure people are doing good-quality jobs, offering decent wages and conditions and reasonable prospects for progression.

Suzy Stride, Labour's prospective parliamentary candidate for Harlow:

'I see the consequences of underemployment and low pay first-hand in Harlow. As expectation for a more skilled and highly trained workforce grows, many people feel left behind because they don't have a skills base to build on and they are failed by the unemployment system. The only option they have left is unemployment or a residual wash-up of insecure low-paid jobs.

Having spent most of my working life up-skilling young people to help them find work, I know how transformative Labour's policy of a jobs guarantee would be. A compulsory job for every unemployed young person would change lives and make a huge difference to people in Harlow and communities across the country.

Raising aspiration among the young and providing good jobs that pay should be the test of any civilised society. Under Labour, they are the backbone of our values and at the centre of our policies.'

The squeeze on hard-working families

Under this government, wages have fallen in real terms – on average, by £1,600 a year. More than one in five workers now earn less than a living wage, and half of all households living below the poverty line have someone in work.

Too many people are stuck on insecure zero-hour contracts, or doing part-time hours when they want to work full-time. There is a growing sense that steady jobs and secure careers are now getting harder to come by and, for too many people, far out of reach.

One mum I met recently told me how she struggled to survive and provide for her young son with her minimum wage job – shopping at cheaper supermarkets, cooking food in bulk quantities and freezing it, touring car boot sales and charity shops. 'You cut all your out-goings', she said, but still you find yourself having to make choices about giving your child 'a nutritious dinner'. No one in work should ever have to make that choice.

Another family I visited had thought they were doing OK, with their own house and kids doing well at school. But since the father's small business failed in the recession he had only been able to get work through employment agencies, often on zero-hour contracts, while the mother had to give up her plans to train to be a primary school teacher and keep up her job in retail so they didn't fall behind with the mortgage payments. Their biggest worry was what the future held for their children. Their daughter's Saturday job barely paid enough to cover her bus fare. She was hoping to go to university but worried about covering her living costs and paying the fees.

Matthew Pennycook, Labour's prospective parliamentary candidate for Greenwich and Woolwich:

'Knock on almost any door in my constituency of Greenwich and Woolwich and you'll find people struggling to make ends meet, pay their bills, or save for a home. Many feel that no matter how many

jobs they take on or how hard they work, the odds are stacked against
them and their families.

The faltering living standards of those on low and middle incomes is
a longstanding problem. Even in the boom years before 2008, incomes
were faltering for a broad swathe of working households. The prolonged
economic slump this Conservative-led government has overseen has
exacerbated that underlying structural problem.

Addressing the challenge of faltering living standards is the defining challenge of our age. It will not be easy, but only Labour are ready
to meet it.'

Rewards for hard work

We can't succeed as a country if all the gains of economic growth
are concentrated in the hands of a privileged few while increasing
numbers of people feel they are working harder, for longer, for less.
Labour has a comprehensive and coherent plan to turn this around
– making sure that work pays and that good quality, well-paying jobs
offering security, satisfaction and a sustainable career are not seen
as a thing of the past but as something to which everyone can aspire.

A Labour government will restore the link between hard work and
fair reward, so that all working people have a chance to share in the
prosperity they help to create.

We will take action in five main areas:

First, Labour will set an ambitious target for the national minimum wage so that it rises relative to average earnings over the
lifetime of the next parliament, and toughen up enforcement with
higher fines for companies who fail to pay it. Labour will work closely
with employers to tackle the barriers to raising skills, productivity,
pay and progression in sectors such as retail, hospitality and social care.

Second, Labour will introduce 'Make Work Pay' contracts to
encourage more companies to commit to paying all their employees a

'living wage' by sharing with them some of the savings that result for the Treasury when those workers are less reliant on benefits and tax credits. That is a good deal for firms who want to do the right thing, a good deal for their staff who will get a pay rise, and a good deal for taxpayers who will see a lower social security bill over the long term.

Alan Buckle, former deputy chairman at KPMG International and author of the independent report 'Low Pay: The National Challenge' for Labour's Policy Review:

'I know from a thirty-year business career that decent pay is good for business: lower staff turnover, great loyalty, high productivity and a better place to work. Since 2010, the almost six million people who earn below the living wage have seen their pay rises fail to keep up with inflation. They are hit hardest by the rises in rent, energy and food prices. This group is also hit hardest by a decline in public services.

My report on low pay recommended a national campaign over five years – including employers, unions and government – to take the national minimum wage to a far higher level. The minimum wage will move closer to the average and when times get tough, those who are less well-off will be protected. I recommended a clamp-down on non-payment of the minimum wage and strong support for a living wage.

This is a triple win: for the low-paid, for taxpayers – because higher pay means lower benefit payments and more people sharing the tax burden – and for our economy, and only Labour will deliver it.'

John Hannett, General Secretary of the Union of Shop, Distributive and Allied Workers (Usdaw) and member of the Low Pay Commission:

'Many working people have found themselves having to work harder for less than average pay since 2010. Usdaw members are only too well aware that there is a difference between a Labour government and the Tory-led government.

The current government is hell-bent on an ideological attack on the cost of living and on workers' rights. That is in contrast to a future Labour government committed to ensuring working people will see more of what they earn, enforcing the minimum wage properly so that it protects the most vulnerable.

The national minimum wage was one of Labour's greatest achievements but it has been devalued by the current government. Only a Labour government is committed to fairness, making work pay and to ensuring the minimum wage will rise in real terms.'

Third, Labour will crack down on dodgy agencies and discriminatory employment practices. As David Hanson and Polly Billington discuss further in their chapter, Labour will ensure that the exploitation of migrant workers can't be used as a way of undercutting and undermining everyone's wages and working conditions.

Fourth, Labour will end the abuse of zero-hour contracts – protecting workers against unfair exclusivity rules or no-notice shift cancellations and giving them a right to have their regular working hours properly reflected in their contract.

Alison McGovern, Labour Member of Parliament for Wirral South:

'Exploitative zero-hour contracts have become an unwelcome way of life for so many of my constituents. Such contracts are good news for the government, because it gets unemployment figures down, but for too many people they fail to provide the security of income that ought to come with having a job.

Zero-hour contracts can provide flexibility that works for some people, but far too often I hear complaints about favouritism in providing work, notice of work availability that is too short to arrange childcare or unacceptable exclusivity clauses that stop employees topping up their unpredictable incomes through other work.

The government have failed to match Labour's plan to outlaw exploitation of zero-hour contracts. Only a Labour government will protect people so they are not forced to be available around the clock and have the power to demand a regular contract if they are working regular hours.'

Norman Pickavance, former HR and Communications Director at Morrisons PLC, author of an independent consultation on zero-hour contracts for Labour's Policy Review:

'Britain's future success is reliant on a highly skilled, highly motivated and highly adaptive workforce. Yet every indicator shows Britain has weak skills levels compared to our global competitors, declining levels of employee engagement and increasing levels of workplace stress. Why is this?

The root cause lies in a limited outlook held by some companies in how they view their own people. Far from being their biggest asset, many employees are increasingly made to feel like a disposable resource, hired on contracts which do not provide either a shared sense of commitment or any kind of security on which people can plan their lives.

The exploitation of work practices like zero-hour contracts reflect the erosion of a basic foundation on which so much else in life is built. The workplace is a reflection of the kind of society we all want to live in, one in which everyone is treated with dignity and respect and can build a stable and fulfilling life. It is for these reasons that I have recommended that the use of zero-hour and similar contracts, as a way of structuring long-term work relationships, must be curtailed.'

Fifth, these radical reforms will go hand-in-hand with the plans set out elsewhere in this chapter and book to raise the skill levels, productivity and earning power of British workers, and support and secure investment in the ideas, innovation and new industries that can create more high-quality, high-skilled, well-paying jobs in every part of the country.

A rising national minimum wage; encouraging a living wage; a crack-down on dodgy agencies which exploit migrants; an end to zero-hour contracts; a skills revolution. These are the policies which will make work pay for you and your family.

Recognising and rewarding contribution

Part of an economy that works for working people is a system of social security and pension provision that recognises and rewards the contribution that people make over their working lives.

The welfare state was built on the principle of pooling resources and sharing risks, with everyone contributing when they can, so that everyone can count on support when they fall on hard times, and then look forward to a decent and dignified retirement when they reach pension age.

A Labour government will renew and reinforce this principle, by recognising and rewarding the contributions people make to the social security system, and ensuring they can count on a decent state pension as well as contribute to a workplace pension that gives them good value for money for their savings.

For the state pension we support the 'triple lock' which means its value is protected, rising in line with prices, earnings or 2.5 per cent, whichever is higher. Labour will pursue all necessary reforms to ensure that working people can save into a workplace pension without worrying that their pension pot will be eaten up by hidden fees and charges and secure in the knowledge that they will be able to turn it into a decent and reliable retirement when they reach the end of their working life.

A Labour government will also increase the rate of contributory Jobseeker's Allowance that people receive for an initial period after losing their job, which we'll fund by increasing the length of time people need to have been working and making national insurance contributions to qualify. Migrant workers will be unable to claim out-of-work benefits until they have worked in the UK for six months.

Fran's story

Two years ago I met Fran, a mother of two who worked in a canteen to support her children. She had recently been involved in a successful campaign to win a living wage for herself and her co-workers. She described the difference it had made to her family. Her two children are keen and talented basketball players who competed in local tournaments. Now she could afford to buy them proper shoes to play in – and go to the matches to watch them.

We need a government that is on the side of hard-working mums like Fran, on the side of young people who are keen to get started on a career and are ready to put in the effort but need some help to brush up their skills or find the right path; on the side of everyone who wants their job to be something they are proud to do well, as well as something that allows them to build a decent life for themselves and their families.

We need a Labour government that will get our country to work – so that together we can all build an economy that works for working people.

Rachel Reeves is the Member of Parliament for Leeds West and shadow Secretary of State for Work and Pensions.

SECTION 2

AN INCLUSIVE SOCIETY

Society is made up of individuals and their relationships, and family in all its varied forms is its bedrock. An inclusive society is based on a mutual recognition that we are all dependent upon other people throughout our lives. It values reciprocity which establishes a sense of justice in relationships: 'Do not do to others what you would not have them do to you.' Its institutions promote the power of relationships to transform people's lives, and to strengthen the capabilities of men, women and children for resilience, love and care.

Central government over the last thirty years has not been able to answer the social problems of our time such as loneliness, growing inequality, family breakdown, loss of community, rising mental ill health, and care for older people. People are losing confidence in the ability of our public institutions to serve the common good of society. In a time when there is no money to spare, we need big reform not big spending.

Creating an inclusive society is at the heart of Labour's programme for national renewal. We will redefine the relationship between government and individuals by reforming the state and sharing more power and responsibility with people. We will help people to help themselves so that they can play a more active role in solving their own problems.

We will increase the power of local communities by building collaboration among public services and organisations, and pooling funds to stop inefficiency and avoid duplication. Designing policy will involve people as genuine partners in shaping their services around their individual needs. And we will invest to prevent social problems from developing and so save money in the future.

An inclusive society thrives with self-confident citizens. It will grow by helping children to develop the emotional skills, self-esteem and relationships they need to live flourishing lives.

Jon Cruddas MP is Coordinator of Labour's Policy Review.

Chapter 4

Supporting Modern Families

LUCY POWELL MP

'A happy family is but an earlier heaven.'

— George Bernard Shaw

Family relationships are the bedrock of our society. Families are the foundation for healthy, active, aspirational citizens who contribute to local communities, the economy and the good of the country.

In the past, Labour has too often shied away from advocating for families, even as we have put them at the heart of our agenda for tackling poverty, increasing social mobility and giving every child the best start in life. Today we embrace our proud record of supporting families, putting them at the centre of our plans to shape public services and our economy.

Labour is the party of the family. Ours is not some narrow backward view of what a family should look like; we are the party that understands and supports the needs of all families, in whatever shape and size they come.

Labour in office has a particularly proud record: a year's maternity leave; the right to request flexible working; massive expansion of early years education; more childcare; tax credits and vouchers to help meet costs; free early education for three- and four-year-olds;

Sure Start children's centres in every community with the ambition to support families and children.

Supporting families is a key part of Ed Miliband's One Nation agenda. At the heart of this is the question of how we see the role of the state in the lives of families. Strong families are built on strong relationships; a strong country and strong economy are built on the relationship between the state and the family. So the question for us is how we use the limited resources we have to get the most benefit for families, society and the economy.

Our starting point must be that all parents instinctively want to do the best for their children. Parents want to ensure their children have the best start, that they are protected from harm and neglect, and given the social and educational tools to succeed as they grow and develop. Yet we know for some parents there are barriers to this loving instinct.

Whether these are personal barriers created by difficult issues in their own childhood, or societal factors such as poverty, worklessness or physical and mental ill health, for some parents and children the state must step in to give protection, nurture and support.

For others, factors like high childcare costs, poor housing costs or low skills can act as a barrier to opportunity, getting into work, providing enough for a family, and for getting on in life.

At the next election, Labour will renew our commitment to all families and ensure that we give parents the tools to be the best parents they can, breaking down the barriers that cause inequality and strengthening opportunity and aspiration.

Life is getting harder for families

For many parents, balancing work and family life has become increasingly difficult. The structure of families has fundamentally changed over the last twenty years. Public policy has failed to keep up with these changes. In 1996, 71 per cent of families with dependent children were headed by a married couple. By 2008 this was 60 per cent. While there has been a quiet revolution in the way people live their lives, we haven't seen the revolution in family policy to match.

Today there are more women than ever in work. There are more women who want to work and more who need to work. A third of all mothers with dependent children now earn the majority share of household income. Indeed, as the Joseph Rowntree Foundation has shown, single-breadwinner households today are more likely to be in poverty. Gone are the days of dad working while mum stays at home bringing up the kids. While this is the choice of some, it is not the reality for the majority. More and more dads also want to play an active role in their children's upbringing. Families need to work more hours and more anti-social hours to make ends meet, but are also struggling for the time and space to enjoy their kids.

High childcare costs mean second earners – invariably women – find it harder than ever to make work pay. Take the mums I met with Ed Miliband at the Co-operative Childcare's Wythenshawe nursery in Manchester in February this year. They were particularly vexed that they got no help when returning to work and feel penalised for doing the right thing. They want to work but often those first few steps back to the job market can be difficult because the cost and availability of childcare is a major barrier for many mums with pre-school children.

For dads these days too, taking that active role in their children's lives has become more difficult. That's why Labour brought in paid paternity leave and the right to flexible working, and why I support the government's introduction of shared parental leave.

Without a cultural shift in the workplace, men will continue to have requests turned down and leave won't be taken. Dads are less likely to ask for flexible working and are twice as likely to be turned down than women; just 1 per cent of eligible dads have taken additional paternity leave, suggesting that government estimates of the number of dads who will sign up for shared parental leave are overly optimistic. We won't see the shift families want under the current government policy.

As many mums and dads will tell you, the most important job they do is to bring up happy and confident children. But they also do important and worthwhile jobs which keep the economy moving and contribute to the country.

Yet family policy doesn't match parental ambition – mums' and dads' choices remain constrained.

As Rachel Reeves outlined in her chapter, parents are working harder, for longer and for less money under this government. There are increasing pressures on family budgets and on family time. Childcare costs have rocketed since 2010, with nursery costs rising five times faster than wages. This is a problem for families because some parents don't know if they will be better off in work at the end of the month, after they have accounted for childcare costs, or not. It is also a problem for the economy as women particularly are trapped out of work because the childcare crunch is too difficult to solve.

Under this government we have seen a hollowing out of services that provide vital support and strong foundations for families. By the end of this parliament, £15 billion will have been taken away from support for families. On top of this, services have been slashed. Despite promises from the Prime Minister and Deputy Prime Minister about protecting Sure Start, we've seen over 600 fewer centres as well as reductions in services and staff. This infrastructure offering support, and sign-posting families that need it for extra support, is being eroded at a time when pressures on families are greater. Sure Start is one of Labour's greatest success stories. Behind the overall story of achievement lie so many tales of individual families getting the support they needed at the right time.

For example, I recently met a young mother in Manchester whose children would have been taken into care if it weren't for the 'tough love' of an outreach worker. The outreach worker supported her to improve her parenting, gain confidence as a mother and set herself on the path to training and work. The outreach worker kept coming to her house, pushing and supporting her to become stronger and more confident as a parent. This was part of Manchester City Council's pioneering joined-up approach to revitalising Sure Start, which brings together midwives, health visitors and outreach workers to identify parents and babies in need and give them early help.

At the same time the programmes the government ministers have championed have flopped precisely because the services that might have sign-posted parents to them have been decimated. The government's free parenting classes trial has helped just 5 per cent of the eligible population; their relationship support trial had fewer than ten applications across all of the pilot areas; and plans to sign up new parents for help and advice through pregnancy and childbirth have been shunned by three-quarters of new parents.

Dame Tessa Jowell MP, former Public Health Minister who led on the creation of Sure Start centres during the last Labour government:

'Sure Start was important when it was established as an early nurture programme in 2000. We now know even more, from the evidence of early childhood development, that it is an indispensable facility for some of our poorest children in our constant fight against inequality and the lack of social mobility.

Sure Start can help mothers and fathers learn how to be their child's first teacher and to understand the importance of language, singing and constant nurturing communication. It can also provide the much-needed affordable and flexible childcare which means working parents can match the demands of employment and the need for a regular income, with the developmental needs of their children who they love more than anything else in the world.

Sure Start was seen as almost untouchable in 2010. All parties rushed to reaffirm their commitment to it. The fact is that since the Tory-led government was elected, we have seen over 600 Sure Start centres close and those children and their families impoverished as a result.'

Labour's vision for families and children

The Labour vision for families and children recognises the changing nature of families today. Our policies and plans support the extended family contributing to the lives of children. We also recognise and strongly support the growing consensus that intervening early can transform futures.

We know that the first years of life are vital to a child's future life chances. By preventing poor outcomes later in life through effective early intervention we can make a difference for families and communities, as well as reducing the burden of failed families on the state.

Labour is committed to the principles and practices of Sure Start as a key early intervention tool to support parents and children. Labour will look to revitalise the fractured system of Sure Start we inherit by renewing our commitment to the core principle to which it aspires: early help for any family that needs it.

To fulfil the promise of the next generation, Labour will build a new vision for children's centres. To genuinely make a difference we need to see a shift in resource: an 'invest early to save later' culture that will reap dividends for families and the exchequer. Labour's Local Government Innovation Taskforce has recently backed this vision. It recommends Sure Start centres should become hubs of support for children and families. Local services for health and family support co-operating and co-locating to provide a single point of access in every community. I know from where this is working in Manchester what a transformational impact it can have. It is my starting point for the renewal of Sure Start.

On childcare, too, Labour is working to ensure high-quality early education and childcare are available, to close the social mobility and developmental gap that exists between the poorest children and their peers.

High-quality flexible childcare is also part of the solution to some of the key challenges facing families and our country. Our maternal employment rates, particularly for mothers with children aged one to four are poor when compared with other OECD countries. Childcare is a barrier to growing the economy and boosting maternal employment.

Over a third of mothers want to work but are unable to as a result of high childcare costs. Two-thirds of mothers would like to work more hours but are unable to do so because taking on more hours means higher childcare bills. Throw in zero-hour contracts, short-hour shifts and atypical working, and it is easy to see how many parents are trapped at home because they can't find the right childcare to meet their needs.

The Institute for Public Policy Research (IPPR) has shown convincingly that investment in childcare reaps fiscal benefits as well as helping more mothers into work. A 10 per cent increase in maternal employment rates could boost the exchequer by £1.5 billion a year, not just helping government finances but family finances too.

Childcare can also help us tackle gender inequality and the motherhood pay penalty. Too many mothers still face a pay and status penalty in the labour market for having children. Pregnancy discrimination, inflexible working opportunities and a lack of affordable childcare all hold back the career chances and family choices of parents. A more comprehensive childcare system integrated with family-friendly working practices would also enable more dads to play the role they want and free more women to succeed at work as well as at home.

While the gender pay gap is negligible for young professional women, for mothers the gap is stark. The pay gap between what men and women earn in work has increased in the last five years for the first time. It is a waste of potential that so many women leave the labour market after having children, never to return to the same job with equal pay and status.

This is borne out by figures which show that men enjoy an extra decade of pay rises, with earnings peaking in their fifties, while women see wages fall from their thirties. This significant widening of the gap can be put down to women leaving the labour market to have children and combined with the fact that many will never regain their prior pay and status.

Women are still failing to get through the glass ceiling and to the top of companies after having children, with earnings stalling at the moment they should be surging ahead. We should do more to value part-time and flexible workers, particularly working mothers. Working parents have often done a day's work before they even get to work and are some of the most productive and loyal employees. We need to see a cultural shift which values working parents if we're to tackle the barriers they face.

Improved childcare and sharing care with partners could ease this burden, reduce the pay gap and let women have an equal chance at a successful career and home life.

Paula Sherriff, Labour's prospective parliamentary candidate in Dewsbury:

'In Dewsbury, women in full-time positions still earn under £100 less per week than men. That's a shocking statistic. National figures show that women in full-time work earn over 15 per cent less than men in equivalent roles. The last Labour government closed the pay gap by 7.7 per cent, but under David Cameron it is widening again.

Many women I have met have told me how they have found themselves trapped in lower-paid positions, or even worse. One young mum spoke about being forced out of her job after taking maternity leave to have her daughter. That's too much potential being wasted for any political party to ignore.

We should be working with trade unions, businesses and local authorities for greater pay transparency, challenging bad practices where we find them, and celebrating employers that take their responsibilities seriously and deal with female workers on a truly fair and equal basis.'

Childcare and early years education boosting social mobility

High quality childcare is good for society as well as families. It can close the developmental gap and equip children with the skills and experiences they need to be successful in school and later life. Quality childcare can lay the foundations for our country's future and be a key tool in our early-intervention armoury. While many childcare settings provide good quality care, there is room for improvement.

We know that many of the most disadvantaged can start school eighteen months behind their peers. Quality childcare settings can help but we should also work to empower parents to be involved in their children's learning.

We spend huge public resources trying to redress these gaps later on, in the education system and other areas. Surely reducing this gap earlier would prove to be a more effective intervention.

Labour's offer to families

Labour's extension of free childcare from fifteen to twenty-five hours a week will be a huge boost to parents, helping them to make informed choices about going back to work.

Under our plans, second earners will, for the first time, be able to go back to work part-time without having to worry about childcare costs. Labour's extra childcare provision for working mums and dads is worth £1,500 per year per child and is on top of government plans for tax-free childcare.

To tackle the logistical nightmare faced by parents, Labour will also lay down in law a 'primary childcare guarantee' so parents of primary school children are guaranteed access to before- and after-school care for their children at their local primary school or nearby. This will give parents trying to juggle working life with childcare outside of school hours the reassurance they need. So Labour has a strong and ambitious childcare offer to parents in 2015.

These costed proposals are an important and major step forwards in improving childcare support for families. Labour in government will continue to develop a comprehensive platform to meet parental aspiration and ambition. In the same way we make the economic case for infrastructure projects, Labour will show that childcare isn't an optional extra but fundamental to our future prosperity.

Will Martindale, Labour's prospective parliamentary candidate for Battersea, the youngest constituency in the country:

'As a young dad myself, I know the difference that good-quality, affordable childcare can make. Battersea is home to many young families like mine, but childcare costs have jumped by 30 per cent in just three years. I've met parents in tears on the doorstep because they are desperate to use the skills and the qualifications they worked for, but childcare costs make it impossible. Many of them feel the time away from their family is just not worth it.

We need to change the way we think about childcare and make sure parents get the support they need to have both fulfilled family lives and careers.'

Tulip Siddiq, Labour's prospective parliamentary candidate for Hampstead and Kilburn:

'Around a third of the nine million people who rent are families with children, but many families can no longer afford to live in places like Queen's Park in my constituency. House prices are rising faster than anywhere else in London and people are having to spend more than 50 per cent of their salary on rent. Teachers, nurses and policemen are being priced out.

With many in the private rented sector on a default six-month contract, many families live knowing they could have to move with just two months' notice. This is incredibly destabilising and all the more difficult to plan a family budget.

That's why Ed Miliband's pledge to make three-year tenancies the norm in the private rental sector and end unpredictable rent increases is so important. It will give stability to families across the country and make sure people from all walks of life can continue to live in diverse communities like mine.'

Labour's family policy priorities will reflect the changing nature of parenting. Family-friendly employment practices should dovetail with childcare plans, so parents are offered seamless support when they need it most at the key transition points in family life, whether that is preparing to have a baby, thinking about returning to work after parental leave, or their children's transition to school.

More dads want to take a role in their child's life while, in the absence of good childcare, grandparents and other family members too are contributing to help parents balance work and family life.

The IPPR has called for measures in their *Condition of Britain* report to better support fathers to be more involved from the beginning. They show that a 'use it or lose it' period of 'daddy leave' can help fathers bond with their babies and support their partners.

Labour will look at how best to support fathers' involvement with their children subject to funds being identified. The evidence shows that this is critical to children's development and also vital to build strong couple relationships that last. We support the extension of flexible working to all workers and I hope this will enable a shift that supports grandparents to play a family role without leaving the labour market.

Conclusion: meeting modern families' aspirations

Family is at the heart of One Nation Labour politics. Tackling the inequalities that exist within and between families, the state and society will be an important part of Ed Miliband's pledge to fulfil the promise of Britain.

In office, Labour will work to put the aspirations and ambitions of modern families at the heart of our policy-making so that policy breaks down barriers facing families so they can succeed. The economy and public services do not work for some parents. Labour will embrace reform and deliver the real change that families need to reach their potential at home and at work.

Our One Nation vision of strong families at the heart of stable, prosperous communities will deliver for parents and children and for Britain.

Lucy Powell is the Member of Parliament for Manchester Central and the shadow Minister for Children and Childcare.

Chapter 5

Living Longer, Healthier and Happier Lives

LIZ KENDALL MP

'[The NHS] is regarded all over the world as the most civilised achievement of modern government.'

—Aneurin Bevan

It is the winter of 1996, in the dog days of John Major's government, and the NHS is in crisis.

People are being left on A&E trolleys for hours at a time. Patients are waiting months or even years for vital treatment, and operations are regularly cancelled. Older people are stuck on hospital wards because cuts to social care mean they can't get the care they need in the community or at home. Years without investment have left NHS buildings crumbling and hospitals are projecting deficits as they struggle to balance the books.

This crisis in the NHS led some people to ask if it could survive as a universal tax-funded service, free at the point of use, but by the end of Labour's thirteen years in government the question had been answered with a resounding 'yes'.

Labour's NHS record

Through investment and reform, Labour transformed the NHS and patient satisfaction was at an all-time high. Waiting times were reduced from more than eighteen months to a maximum of eighteen weeks. There were more doctors and nurses than ever before and hospitals were rebuilt or refurbished. Guaranteed waiting times and extended surgery opening hours made it easier for people to see a GP. New primary care centres, pharmacy services and walk-in centres improved access to NHS services in the community.

Alongside better access to services, Labour drove improvements in the quality of care through expert cancer and stroke networks, by publishing information on stroke and heart care outcomes and by introducing the first ever independent regulation of the NHS and social care.

Patients got more power and control through new rights in the NHS Constitution (including to choose their GP and hospital), better information (such as NHS Choices), and by introducing personal budgets in social care for older and disabled people.

Mental healthcare improved, with talking therapies and new crisis intervention teams in the community. Unpaid family carers got new rights and breaks from their caring responsibilities, and national strategies for dementia and end-of-life care put these issues on the agenda for the first time.

Labour took bold action on public health too. Concerted action to tackle health inequalities in 'spearhead' communities helped narrow the gap in male life expectancy between the poorest and richest areas. Inequalities in infant mortality fell, teenage pregnancy rates were reduced and Labour's ban on smoking in public places is saving tens of thousands of lives.

These huge achievements on the NHS forced the Tories onto Labour's ground. Before he became Prime Minister, David Cameron said his priorities could be summed up in three letters: NHS. In his 2010 general election poster, Cameron promised to 'cut the deficit, not the NHS'. He also pledged that 'there will be no more of the tiresome, meddlesome, top-down restructures that have dominated the last decade of the NHS'.

Four years on, patients and the public have seen these promises broken. Far from protecting the NHS, vital services have been cut and patient care is going backwards. We are fast heading back to the crisis I described at the start of this chapter, when John Major was Prime Minister.

Andy Burnham MP, shadow Health Secretary:

'This coming election will determine the future of our National Health Service. Labour will restore the right values to the heart of our NHS: integration over fragmentation; collaboration over competition; people before profits. Labour will create an NHS for the whole person. We will build a single service able to meet all of one person's needs – physical, mental and social.

The choice before the country at the next election couldn't be clearer: a privatised health system under Cameron, or a revitalised public NHS under Labour.'

The reorganisation no one wanted

David Cameron's single biggest mistake in government was to force through the biggest reorganisation in the history of the NHS, when the NHS faced the biggest financial challenge of its life. This has wasted three years of effort and energy, and £3 billion of taxpayers' money which should have gone on improving patient care.

The Prime Minister claimed his reorganisation would put clinicians in charge, when his goal should have been giving patients more power and control. David Cameron hasn't even succeeded in putting GPs in the driving seat, because his reorganisation has created even more layers of bureaucracy as well as chaos and confusion in the system.

Four-hundred and forty new organisations have been created in total. These include not only 221 local Clinical Commissioning Groups, 152 local Health and Wellbeing Boards and the huge new national quango NHS England, but four new regional NHS England teams, twenty-seven Local Area Teams and nineteen Specialist Commissioning Units. Alongside Public Health England, Health Education England, Monitor and the Care Quality Commission, the NHS is now so complex that no one knows who is responsible or accountable for leading the changes to front-line services that patients and taxpayers so desperately need.

The waste of time and money on the reorganisation, combined with the fragmentation and confusion it has created, means the NHS is now going backwards.

Jamie Reed MP, shadow Health Minister:

'Having promised not to reorganise the NHS before the 2010 general election, David Cameron has inflicted the largest top-down reorganisation the NHS has ever seen. These reforms have mandated local commissioners to outsource services to the private sector, insisted that hospitals increase their revenues by imposing a private patient quota of 49 per cent and laid the foundations for the privatisation of the National Health Service.

The tragedy of this is that, at the same time these changes were being introduced, independent international bodies such as the Commonwealth Fund, using data from the NHS left behind by the last Labour government, found that the NHS was the best, most efficient health service in the world.

It is patients who have felt the brunt of Cameron's ideological vandalism and it will again be left to the next Labour government to rebuild the NHS. We will repeal the Tories' damaging market-driven health policies and introduce an integrated system of care across NHS, community health and adult services that places the needs of the patient at the centre of health service provision.'

The challenges facing our NHS

Hospital A&Es have failed to meet the government's lower four-hour waiting target in every single week of the last year. Over the last twelve months, a million more people have waited for more than four hours in casualty departments.

Rising emergency admissions mean planned operations are going backwards too. Three million people are now waiting for an operation, average waits for operations are increasing, and cancelled operations are at their highest level for a decade. For the first time ever, the NHS has missed the maximum 62-day wait for cancer treatment, with twice as many NHS trusts overshooting the target in 2014 compared to 2013.

It is also getting harder to see your local GP. The Tories scrapped Labour's forty-eight-hour guarantee; now almost two-thirds of patients say they cannot see their doctor within two days. One in six people have to wait more than a week to see their GP, an increase of 1.3 million people since 2011/12. GP surgeries are shutting their doors earlier because the Tories scrapped Labour's incentives for more convenient opening hours, and walk-in centres have been closed across the country.

Huge cuts to social care are piling further pressure on local hospitals. Since 2010, £3.5 billion has been cut from local council care budgets and a quarter of a million fewer people are now getting vital services like home care visits, which help elderly people get up, washed, dressed and fed.

Too little help in the community and at home means increasing numbers of elderly people are ending up in A&E and getting stuck in hospital when they don't need to be there. This causes huge distress for them and their families, and is a false economy as taxpayers end up paying extra for more expensive hospital care.

The NHS is facing a growing financial crisis too. Trusts as a whole ended 2013/14 in deficit: the first time in eight years. One in three hospital trusts are now in the red and two-thirds of trusts that have gone into deficit have done so since the general election.

The Tories, backed up by the Liberal Democrats, are undoing the progress that Labour made and it is patients, their families and taxpayers who are paying the price.

Heidi Alexander, Labour MP for Lewisham East:

'The public are right to want their say on how the NHS is organised and they are right to demand that changes to services must always be driven by what is in the best interest of patients.

Attempts to ram through closures at well-performing hospitals to solve financial problems in other parts of the NHS are just wrong. But that is precisely what the Tory–Lib Dem government tried to do in Lewisham. They wanted to take an axe to Lewisham's A&E and maternity department to ease financial pressures elsewhere. When the courts said 'no', they changed the law.

It was the Save Lewisham Hospital Campaign and Labour MPs who stood up to government when they legislated to fast-track hospital closures. People deserve a proper say about the NHS. The new hospital closure law needs to be scrapped and Labour is the only party to do it.'

As the standard of local NHS and care services regresses and with a looming funding crisis, it falls once again to Labour to sustain and renew the NHS.

Dealing with the current crisis, and preparing the NHS for the future, means reforming front-line services to meet the challenges of today and tomorrow: our ageing population; the huge increase in long-term health conditions; changing public expectations and the explosion of new medicines and technologies.

Reforming the NHS for new times

Four big changes are now essential.

First, services must be fully joined up to improve people's experience of care and make better use of taxpayers' money. The experience of places like Torbay has shown that integrating health and social care stops people having to deal with lots of different services and telling their story time and time again. It also cuts the number of emergency bed days, decreases delayed transfers from hospital and reduces the number of people requiring nursing care homes.

Local NHS and council budgets and services must be joined up to make sure every pound of public spending is used to get the best outcomes for users and the best value for money. Joined-up budgets would create the potential for truly integrated care, including one point of contact, one care co-ordinator and one team to meet all of a person's care and support needs. High-quality, integrated care also needs integrated information: on patients' needs, treatment, experiences and outcomes.

Sir John Oldham, former National Clinical lead at the Department of Health and chairman of the Independent Commission on Whole Person Care:

'The NHS in 2014 is facing a very different disease challenge from the one that existed at its inception in 1948. Broadly, the main challenge in 1948 was infectious disease; now it is people with multiple long-term conditions, poor mental health, disabilities and frailty. We can all celebrate the success of rising life expectation, yet because most of us are living longer, the next fifty years will see a growth of at least two and a half times as many people suffering from multiple problems.

The consequences become clearer when thinking about the case of a woman called Mrs P. She is widowed and lives on her own a few miles away from her daughter. She is eighty-five, has breathing problems, high blood pressure and diabetes. In a good month she will typically see ten different professionals from the health and social care world – each of whom has a specific task.

Mrs P went to A&E five times last year. On two occasions she had to be admitted to hospital for breathing trouble because the various elements of care did not help to identify early deterioration. In total she spent thirty days in hospital in emergency beds. This is what happens to millions of people as a result of our fragmented system of care.

It would be better for Mrs P if she saw fewer people who were better-coordinated and better-informed about her care and health. This is what we require commissioners and providers of health and social care to achieve: the needs of one person addressed by people acting as one team, from organisations behaving as one system.'

Baroness Denise Kingsmill, author of 'Taking Care – An independent report into working conditions in the Care Sector':

'Care for elderly and disabled people is a major issue for the mid-21st century. We are all likely to live longer and a large number of us will require care in our final years. We would all wish to be cared for by staff who are valued, qualified, committed and treated properly by their employers and the state. The public purse, however, is tight – and increases in taxation are deeply unpopular ... [There are] immediate changes that could be implemented within existing budget constraints, and long-term objectives that will require investment and extra funding. The most likely source of these additional monies would be the integration of health and social care budgets.'

Second, there must be a fundamental shift in the focus of services outside of hospitals, into the community and towards prevention.

Helping people stay healthy and intervening early on to prevent problems deteriorating is essential to improving people's quality of life and to reduce spending on more expensive hospital and residential care.

Better GP access is essential for prevention. Labour will give all patients the right to consult a doctor or nurse on the same day, have an appointment at their local surgery on the same day if they need to be seen quickly, have a guaranteed appointment at their GP surgery within forty-eight hours and book an appointment more than forty-eight hours ahead with the GP of their choice. We will help all surgeries achieve these standards by investing an extra £100 million a year in family doctor practices, which could pay for an additional three million GP appointments every year. This will be paid for by cutting back on the bureaucracy and costs of competition created by the government's Health and Social Care Act.

Achieving a fundamental shift towards prevention means changing the existing payment systems in the NHS. These are predominantly based on rewarding episodic treatment of separate health conditions in hospitals, rather than investing in the grab-rail, home-care visit or community nurse that would help frail elderly people remain living at home. A new capitated 'year of care' budget covering the whole of a person's physical, mental and social care needs would help switch the focus, giving a strong incentive to provide better preventive services in the community and at home.

New technologies like smartphones and health apps open up huge possibilities to provide people with personalised health information and advice, and telecare services can support people with long-term illnesses manage their conditions at home. A stronger role for Health and Wellbeing Boards in commissioning services would also enable better links to be made with housing, employment, leisure and community services – all of which are essential to helping people live longer, healthier lives.

Luciana Berger MP, shadow Minister for Public Health:

'Today, too many people are dying before their time because of illnesses that could have been prevented. Our society and our NHS cannot continue to bear the human and financial cost of diseases caused by smoking, untreated mental health conditions, binge drinking and rising levels of obesity.

The Tory-led government has been unwilling to stand up to vested interests and take the bold action that we need. The next Labour government will respect that adults are able to make their own decisions, but we will make it easier for people to make healthy choices, for example through clear food labelling. As children are not often able to exercise their own choices, Labour will be unafraid to intervene decisively to protect their health.

Mental health is just as important as physical health. Labour is placing mental health at the very heart of our plans. Our whole-person approach will bring mental and physical health services together, along with social care, so that everyone with an illness or injury, whether it is a broken leg or depression, gets the help they need.'

Professor Gabriel Scally, public health academic and former Regional Director of Public Health:

'The last Labour government tackled our biggest health problems, putting the needs of children and the necessity of reducing inequalities at the forefront of a comprehensive range of public health interventions. In contrast, the coalition, via their so-called Responsibility Deal, have both bent over backwards to put vested interests ahead of the health of the population and have dismantled and downgraded one of the best public health systems in the world.

We need on so many fronts, economic as well as social, a country where people, and children in particular, can lead long, healthy and fulfilling lives. Only Labour has the policies and commitment to health that will allow us achieve those goals.'

Third, the NHS and social care must support a greater contribution from individuals, their families and communities. Training and education for NHS and care staff must recognise that, for the majority of the time, people and their family carers manage their conditions on their own. Support to assist people to manage their conditions whenever possible must become the default model – moving from doing things *to* people to doing things *with* them.

Stronger networks of local support are needed too. Initiatives like the Neighbourhood Networks in Leeds and the Sandwell Friends and Neighbours project identify volunteers to help elderly and disabled people alongside statutory services. These volunteers provide practical and emotional support, such as going shopping, organising social events, or just being available to talk – things that make a real difference to people's lives but aren't currently being provided. New technology and social media can also help create 'virtual' networks of people with similar conditions and link up family carers, so that they can learn from and better support one another.

Fourth, services must be fully personalised and designed around the needs of individuals and families, rather than those of service providers and their staff. Focusing on what matters most to people can drive fundamental changes in how services are organised, the culture and practice of staff and the quality of users' experiences. Labour will empower people to get personalised care with new rights and entitlements through the NHS Constitution.

Achieving genuinely personalised care means giving people greater power and control. Living day in, day out with a health condition means patients often know best how to prevent it from getting worse. Patients and families also care more about getting the right help than which service or organisation provides it.

Personalised care-planning, where individuals and their families play an active part in determining their own care and support, is essential for people with long-term health conditions.

Personal budgets will also have an important role to play. Personal budgets and direct payments in social care, introduced under the last Labour government, have helped to transform the lives of thousands of disabled people and their families, giving them greater control over vital services that affect their daily lives. Labour also began piloting personal budgets for people with long-term health conditions in 2009. The national evaluation of these pilots has shown that giving individuals choice and control improves their quality of life and well-being and reduces their use of more expensive hospital care.

There are, of course, many aspects of NHS care where a personal health budget will not be suitable, such as emergency and inpatient care. However, for the growing number of people with long-term health conditions, personal budgets are an important way of ensuring a publicly funded health system can do the things people really want.

Labour's proud track record on the NHS, this government's abject failure to protect it, and our plans to renew services so they are fit for the future are central to answering the question 'why vote Labour?'

Wes Streeting, Labour's parliamentary candidate for Ilford North and Cabinet Member for Health & Wellbeing on Redbridge Council:

'As a newly-elected Labour council, Redbridge is working to show residents the difference that voting Labour can make to local health outcomes.

Leisure, culture and lifelong learning services can have a transformational impact on the health and well-being of some of our most at-risk groups if they are designed, targeted and commissioned effectively. That's why we are not only committed to integrating health and social care, but are prioritising these non-statutory services and projects like building a new swimming pool to ensure we're focusing on prevention as much as cure.'

No change is not an option

The NHS is a part of all our lives from the moment we are born to the time we die, and often many times in between. But the NHS is even more than this. It is an expression of our values: our belief in the power of collective action to change people's lives for the better; that care should be available to each of us according to our needs, not our ability to pay; and that power should be in the hands of the many not the few.

It has always been our task as a party to sustain and reform the NHS. Now that task is upon us again.

It won't be easy. NHS and social care staff feel battered and bruised by the huge number of changes that have taken place in recent years. Risks are inherent whenever changes are made. However, the risks of not doing things differently are equally great. No change is not an option.

Bill Clinton once said 'those who believe in government have an obligation to reinvent government to make it work', not least because it is those without power and wealth who bear the brunt when the state and public services fail.

This is the challenge now facing us: to offer a real alternative and genuine hope that the health and care services we all rely on can be sustained for future generations.

Liz Kendall is the Member of Parliament for Leicester West and the shadow Minister for Care and Older People.

Chapter 6

Aspirational Britain: Empowering Young People

BEX BAILEY

'We cannot always build the future for our youth, but we can build our youth for the future.'

— Franklin D. Roosevelt

Growing up, I saw the difference a Labour government made. The Portakabin in my primary school was taken down and new classrooms built. The results in my secondary school improved year after year. My peers were able to travel to college and pay for the books they needed, thanks to the Education Maintenance Allowance. When I started work I was paid the minimum wage and protected from gender discrimination thanks to Labour's national minimum wage Act and new equality laws.

Labour in government got off to a good start. Those older than me benefited from the pledge card commitment, the New Deal for Young People that eradicated long-term youth unemployment until the global financial crash in 2008. Those my age, fearing unemployment after the collapse of Lehman Brothers, had the Future Jobs Fund. These measures were not only hugely successful for the young people they helped but also saved the Treasury money. The coalition government's own review of the Future Jobs Fund found that half of the money spent by the government made its way back to the exchequer in tax receipts and reduced benefit payments.

Sure Start children's centres sprung up in the local area and Child Trust Funds were introduced, both helping new parents to give their children the best possible start in life. Labour gave young people the support and opportunities we needed to reach our full potential. We were making significant progress.

Now the Conservatives are turning back the clock and reversing the progress Labour made. Our opportunities are being snatched away from us and our services are being eroded. For the first time in a long time, it looks like our generation will not be better off than that of our parents. The Future Jobs Fund has been abolished. Youth unemployment is through the roof. Tuition fees have trebled. The national minimum wage has fallen in real terms since 2010.

Around one in five young people around the country are unemployed. Even those lucky enough to have a job are saying they are struggling to pay their bills and rent as, for the first time, the majority of those in poverty are in work.

Britain is going down the wrong path and we need to set it right again.

Ed Miliband is calling for people-powered politics. This is not just a buzz-phrase but an agenda ready to make a huge impact, as Steve Reed describes in his chapter. With a tight budget and five years of Conservative chaos to clean up, the next parliament will not be easy. Labour's vision of putting power in the hands of parents, patients and all public service users will be transformational, while keeping costs to a minimum for the taxpayer.

Young people are integral to this. It is often said that young people are the future. While obviously true, what is missing from the debate is that we are also the present. We have so much to give to the here and now. It is the Labour Party that recognises this and that will never leave young people behind. Only Labour sees giving young people the voice and opportunities they deserve as two sides of the same coin.

At the next election, voters will have a choice: a choice between a Conservative Britain where young people are ignored – left behind in the search for jobs and affordable homes – or a Labour Britain in which we are given the education, opportunities and access to work that we need to fulfil our potential and achieve our aspirations.

Putting young people at the heart of politics

The first step of Labour's people-powered politics has to be to give a voice to young people. Votes at sixteen is an idea whose time has come.

We have seen young people leading the fight back against this coalition's attacks: marching the streets; campaigning against the cuts to services; voting in the Scottish independence referendum; and joining the Labour Party in huge numbers. Yet despite the huge impact that politics has on them, sixteen- and seventeen-year-olds still go without a voice at election time. The Labour Party will change that.

Stephen Twigg MP, shadow Minister for Political and Constitutional Reform:
'Votes at sixteen is a bold and radical proposal that, hand-in-hand with a renewed commitment to citizenship education, has the potential to energise a new generation of politically active and engaged citizens. Too often we deplore the fact that a majority of young people don't vote in elections but then decide to do nothing about it. Ed Miliband is committed to changing this and the next Labour government will empower young people to ensure their voice is heard.

Youth is not automatically linked to apathy. Young people today are often highly political, with strong opinions on issues affecting their community, families and aspirations. Many don't feel politicians are listening to their concerns or talking about policies that affect them. One important way to confront this malaise is to open up our democratic system to younger people to make sure politicians on all sides listen and take their views into account.'

People say that young people are politically apathetic – and I know many young people who would say this about themselves – yet I have never met a non-political young person. Everyone that I know holds views on political issues: from litter on the street and the local hospital to the education system and matters of peace and war. Politics is part of our daily lives. The problem is that the link between people's daily lives and our political system is often missed. For too many our politics is broken.

Alongside votes at sixteen we need political education in schools to empower young people. A classroom in which children develop their views through debate, are taught how the political system works and learn how they can influence politics to change the world would be a hugely powerful thing.

The measures that Labour is proposing to encourage a higher turnout among young people at the ballot box, such as voter registration in schools, will see young people influencing elections and getting into a habit that will stay with them for life.

We should go further. Rather than closing primary schools to use as polling stations, we should open secondary schools and sixth form colleges as voting stations, allowing people to vote in between lessons. The antiquated idea of only being able to vote at a certain polling station is unhelpful. Supermarkets, town halls, libraries and other buildings should be voting centres for anyone in the constituency, making it easier for young people to vote.

No longer would young people be ignored. A vote in elections, a solid grounding in the issues and a higher turnout among young people will force politicians of all parties to listen to what we have to say and improve their offer to us to win our votes. Labour has the capacity to give young people voice and vision.

A voice for young people in our public services

Giving power to people is not just about voting. Ed Miliband is right to want to give service users control over their services. But it is crucial that this means everyone, including traditionally disengaged groups such as young people.

Young people have been at the harsh end of this government's programme. From day one, the Conservatives, in league with the Liberal Democrats, have carried out a sustained attack on the services on which we rely. Putting power in the hands of young people, as many Labour councils are doing, would be transformational. No longer should services be done *to* our young people but done *by* them and *for* them.

Young people have been fantastic agents of change in public health – important to smoking cessation and obesity reduction. Budgets have rightly been given to local government. While the more 'taboo' parts of public health often go without sufficient advocates, young people and student unions have long been champions of better mental and sexual health services. Youth mayors and student unions should have a voice at the table on local governments' public health bodies. It gives greater meaning to their elections and gives their electors a real say on important public policy issues.

Schools where students co-commission new buildings have seen reductions in bullying and improved performance. Schools where students help recruit the teachers transform learning and see a step change away from bad behaviour. School councils allowed to do more than consult on uniform policy have been involved in radically changing school culture, ethos and attainment.

As UNICEF research has shown,[34] allowing pupils a voice in their

---

34 Gerison Lansdown, 'Promoting children's participation in democratic decision-making', UNICEF, 2001.

education creates a better relationship between staff and pupils and a more effective learning environment. Listening to pupils gives schools an insight into which teaching methods are most effective, how to improve attendance rates and behaviour and whether the curriculum is relevant. When children feel valued and invested in their school, they are more likely to respect it. Education is not just about learning facts and figures, but developing the skills and leadership that can transform communities.

Tristram Hunt MP, shadow Secretary of State for Education:

'William Lovett's chartist schools, Anthony Crosland's comprehensives, Andrew Adonis's sponsored academies – the Labour movement has always harnessed education's emancipatory power in order to deliver social justice and equality of opportunity.

A vote for Labour is a vote for a crusade against social circumstances defining destiny; a vote for unleashing the moral mission and collective endeavour of teaching as the means to guaranteeing all children enjoy the best start in life.

It is a vote for a determined focus on raising basic standards in English and maths (so crucial for later life chances); for finally offering young people a high-quality, high-aspiration vocational education; for nurturing our children's character and well-being as well as their attainment; and for developing a National Baccalaureate to bind different learning pathways together in a rigorous common framework. But most of all it is a vote for ensuring all our children experience the inspiration and wonder of world-class teaching.'

Education is one of the most powerful tools that we have to change society. Under Labour, our classrooms will be at the centre of a cultural revolution. Introducing comprehensive sex and relationship education, as Labour plans to do, would kick start a culture change that reaches far beyond the classroom. Currently, two women a week in the UK are killed by a current or former partner. One in three women worldwide are raped or beaten in their lifetime. Street harassment is so routine that for many women it has become an accepted fact of life. No woman should have to face this and no one should think that it is acceptable. Teaching children from an early age about healthy relationships based on respect and consent, as well as how to recognise the warning signs of abusive relationships, would have a big impact.

Sex and relationship education also has to include teaching about sexuality and gender identity. It was a Labour government that banned the Conservatives' Section 28, which had previously allowed schools to teach that homosexuality was wrong, and it will be a Labour government that continues to promote equality. The levels of homophobic bullying and the normalisation of homophobic language in schools is appalling. It should be made clear that homophobia in schools is not tolerated, and sex and relationship education would go some way towards creating a culture in which sexism and homophobia are challenged and diversity is celebrated.

Giving children the best chances in life also means dramatically improving teaching. A Labour government will drive up standards by ensuring young people are taught by qualified teachers who are constantly developing alongside their pupils. 'Teach First' has had a huge impact, recruiting talented teachers into challenging schools. Now we need 'Teach Next', an organisation that would recruit specialist science and maths teachers from business and industry so that children are learning from exciting role models and can see the potential of studying these subjects. Creating a new culture in teaching, these measures will help to elevate the perception of teaching as a high-status profession.

Real opportunity for the whole, not half

In a world of global competition, we cannot afford to waste the talents of anyone. But under this government, young people have seen tuition fees treble, job opportunities vanish and youth unemployment remains stubbornly high. Now that we are paying £9,000 a year for university tuition, the least we expect is a job at the end of it.

I am currently watching my peers graduating, moving back in with their parents and unable to find jobs. It is certainly not for lack of talent or trying. With the prospect of a Labour government in 2015 comes the promise of a job, which would be guaranteed for any young person out of work for twelve months or more.

The forgotten 50 per cent who do not go to university are not just shut out of the transformational opportunity and high-earning potential that it provides, but too often shut into low-paid jobs and sectors. Apprenticeships and in-work training to help employees up-skill and vacate access jobs in the market can end this divide.

For many, apprenticeships are a fantastic route into work. Sadly, the opportunity is passed up, if seriously considered at all, by many more who do not see the value in them. Too often business leaders talk the talk about apprenticeships but are not prepared to encourage their own children down that route when it comes to it. We need more high-quality apprenticeships, seen not as an inferior option to university but an equal alternative. Labour will deliver this.

Labour will increase the availability and quality of apprenticeships by introducing a universal gold standard, so that we work towards a system where all apprenticeships are Level 3 qualifications and last at least two years. Every firm that wants a major government contract will have to offer apprenticeships. We will also offer employers, working collectively at sector level, a 'something for something' deal – giving them more control over apprenticeship standards and funding. In return, firms will be asked to create new gold standard apprenticeships in their sectors and supply chains.

This approach will create more apprenticeships across all sectors and help us work to end the gender divide in apprenticeships that sees the engineering industry dominated by men and nursing dominated by women. Ending the gender divide within apprenticeships will have exciting ramifications across society, as career paths become determined less by gender and more by skill and interest.

As well as creating more apprenticeships this requires a change of mind-sets in schools. We will require everyone to study maths and English to the age of eighteen and establish a new, gold standard Technical Baccalaureate for sixteen- to nineteen-year-olds. This will include rigorous, stretching and vocational qualifications for the half of young people not planning on going to university. Schools should give as much support to prospective apprentices as they do to prospective university students. Closer links between schools, colleges and employers are critical to this, alongside meaningful and personalised careers advice.

Finally, we will build on the strength of our higher education sector and take technical skills to a new level by introducing new Technical Degrees. These degree-level vocational qualifications will be co-funded, co-designed, and co-delivered by employers and universities, giving young people the chance to get paid in a good job while training for their chosen career.

Aspiration: Labour's hope for a better future

Simon Darvill, chair of Young Labour:
    'Young people have borne the brunt of five years of the Tory-led government. They can't get work, struggle to get on the housing ladder and have had their higher education options hindered by £9,000 fees. Young Labour will be on the front line in the run up to 2015 to ensure Ed Miliband's pledges on the Youth Jobs Guarantee, ending the abuse of zero-hour contracts and building 200,000 new homes a year are heard by the young people of Britain, because they deserve a government who will stand up for them.'

Fionnuala McGoldrick, chair of Labour Students:

'This generation of students and young people feel completely betrayed by this government. We are working harder and all we are getting in return are shrinking life chances. There is a real distrust of politics and it is up to Labour to restore that trust and inspire our generation to believe in a better future.'

Young people, by definition, are the most future-focused voters, but our dreams of a better future are being dashed by this Conservative-led government. Aspiration is at the heart of Labour's values. We believe in social mobility and giving everyone the opportunity to improve their situation. A Labour government will help people to achieve their aspirations.

Young people want to get on the housing ladder. We have seen our parents do it and we have always believed it is something many of us will also do one day. Sadly, that day is looking more and more distant. House prices are rising, the cost of renting is making it hard to save and demand for housing far outstrips supply. Times are tough for those hoping to get on the housing ladder.

The growth we are finally seeing under this government is regionally imbalanced, which especially impacts on young people. We are seeing particularly high house prices in London and the south east, yet not enough jobs outside those same areas. The government's Help to Buy scheme is, in reality, doing little to help in its current form.

The hope of a Labour government remains. Labour will build houses, increasing supply to meet demand. A Labour government will tackle rogue landlords and excessively high rents, allowing people to save some money each month towards a deposit. No more extortionate letting agent fees and unfair evictions at short notice. Instead, tenants will have greater protection, securer tenancies and predictability over their monthly rent payments. This is Labour's promise to all of us who are stuck renting, struggling to save a deposit, and will give us a greater chance of becoming a generation of homeowners, like our parents.

Dr Peter Kyle, Labour's prospective parliamentary candidate for Hove & Portslade and CEO of Working for Youth:

'Britain is being held back by the scourge of youth unemployment because far too many of our young people are unable to make the transition from education to career. It has been a persistent and troubling problem, with solutions ellusive as it requires coordinated action from Whitehall, local government and the private sector.

Labour's Nottingham Council has shown what is possible however through a 'Jobs Pledge', which wisely invests local resources to support small businesses in creating jobs for young people. This is in stark contrast to the government's Youth Contract, which has been such a disaster in getting young people into work that ministers cancelled the programme ahead of schedule.

The school-leavers I speak to in Hove need a Labour government that will provide determined leadership from the centre and work with the private sector to provide them with opportunities and the skills and support they need to take them.'

Labour: the party of young people

By May 2015, we will have endured five years of Tory rule. For five years, the Conservatives will have run roughshod over young people's ambitions. The choice at the next election is clear: a Conservative government that neglects young people or a Labour government that values our contribution and supports us to reach our full potential.

Young people will not be forgotten by a Labour government. Labour is the party of work, the party of aspiration and the party of opportunity. It was the Labour Party that re-built our schools, introduced the minimum wage and gave us the Future Jobs Fund. And it is the Labour Party that, if elected in 2015, will guarantee the young long-term unemployed a job, build the houses we need to get on the property ladder and give sixteen- and seventeen-year-olds a voice in future elections.

Together, this agenda of putting young people at the heart of political, public service and economic change will be radical and of high impact.

A Labour government will change our lives, giving us hope for the future and the chance to transform our present. We have the opportunity to be part of that exciting change. That is why I will be voting for Labour, and why I hope you will too.

Bex Bailey is the elected Youth Representative on Labour's National Executive Committee.

Chapter 7

Getting Immigration Right for Britain

POLLY BILLINGTON &
DAVID HANSON MP

The parliamentary constituencies of Delyn, in north Wales, and Thurrock, in south Essex, where we both live, are over 200 miles apart. You would struggle to find too many similarities between the two places. One is home to London commuters, dockers and hauliers, retail and logistics professionals as well as many entrepreneurs, the other Welsh families, factory workers, farmers and holiday-makers. One sits next to the Thames estuary, the other looks north to the Irish Sea. One constituency, Delyn, has been a Labour-held seat since 1992. The other, Thurrock, has a Conservative majority of just ninety-two, making it one of the most important places for Labour to win back at the election in 2015.

Delyn and Thurrock are as unalike as chalk and cheese, but there is one thing that unites the two places. When we knock on doors in either constituency, as with almost every constituency across the UK, chances are that, before too long, the talk will turn to immigration.

It is easy to see why. Opinion polls now put immigration as one of the top concerns of voters. As such, it is an issue that those who want to run the country need to understand and address. There is no doubt that in the eyes of many voters, who would usually think of themselves as Labour, we have let them down on immigration. If you are one of those voters, this chapter is for you.

Yvette Cooper MP, shadow Home Secretary:

'Labour's approach to immigration has changed. We've listened and learned. We believe immigration has been important for our country over many centuries and will be in the future. But that's also why it needs to be effectively controlled and managed so the system is fair and commands public confidence and consent.

Our guiding principles are about fairness – ensuring we have a system that is good for Britain and for people who live here.

Labour's approach to immigration is a progressive one. Different to the reactionary conservative approach that says all immigration is bad, ramping up the rhetoric, raising false promises and expectations, doing nothing at all about the impact of immigration. Different too to the free market liberal approach which sees immigration purely in terms of market economics: immigrants as a source of innovation, but also as cheap labour to keep wages and inflation low. It is classic laissez-faire, with little regard for the impact on people's lives and any unfair consequences.

We believe we must control immigration with stronger border controls. We must ensure the impact is fair and be tough with those who exploit immigration to undercut local wages and jobs. We must continue our long British tradition of offering sanctuary to refugees fleeing torture and persecution. We reject the divisive politics of the right that promotes hostility instead of building communities and consensus.'

Listening to communities

Concern about immigration comes in many forms. Doorstep conversations turn very quickly to the experience of working people who are already struggling because of the cost-of-living crisis. They tell of insecure jobs being undercut as a result of loopholes in agency worker laws. For too many people protections they took for granted have disappeared as new 'flexibility' makes them slaves to the phone call from the boss who wants you in for just a couple of hours – today.

In some areas, rising levels of immigration have put pressure on local schools, housing or the NHS – pressures which, currently, aren't being sufficiently managed.

In other areas, the pace of change in a community has left people anxious as the place they have lived in all their lives has changed beyond recognition. They are asking basic questions about whether it is fair and right that people who have lived somewhere all their lives are treated exactly the same as people who have only just arrived.

Many share a real worry over how we police our borders to guard against illegal immigration. That is no surprise: the number of people refused entry at British ports and then subsequently deported has fallen by nearly half. The Home Office now remove 10 per cent fewer people who are here illegally and have had asylum applications turned down compared to when Labour was in government in 2010. Only six in 100 reports of illegal immigration result in an investigation and only 1.5 in 100 result in removal.

These anxieties and experiences, especially for those on low incomes, are right at the heart of their concern about living standards and the future of their communities. You only have to talk to Thurrock's dockers and retail workers, whose professions have felt the brunt of casualisation. They see new developments on their doorstep, like Britain's new hi-tech shipping port at London Gateway, and worry how many of the jobs it creates will go to local people.

People aren't stupid. They recognise that there are different kinds of immigration. They know there are many people across the country whose livelihoods depend on the thousands of UK business that need skilled people to come here to work. The Toyota plant in north Wales for example is absolutely reliant on world-class engine designers and engineers from many different countries. Without them, cars wouldn't be made and the plant couldn't sustain thousands of jobs for local people. Since the Tory-led government came to power, many universities have seen fewer foreign students, with the first national drop in numbers in twenty-nine years. However, this means those universities can afford fewer security guards, catering staff and administrators. Those are jobs that are normally filled by people from the local area.

A future Labour government will ensure that Britain thrives in the twenty-first century, and this means we will work to take advantage of all the talents available to us. Why wouldn't we want the UK to have access to the best doctors, engineers and entrepreneurs? But alongside that, the system must be fair and balanced for the people already here. We will act in Britain's interests, address people's genuine and deep concerns, and do this in accordance with our values.

Our patriotism is both inclusive and traditional; it encompasses successful Brits like Mo Farah who have been part of the story of immigration to the UK, and Great British success stories like Tesco and Marks & Spencer, which were both founded by entrepreneurs descended from Eastern Europe. But it also offers a future to those who are concerned about immigration and currently feel that the chances for success are disappearing out of view, for themselves and for their children.

This is a basic argument about equality of opportunity, as well as economic prosperity, which is at the heart of what Labour is about as a party. It means that we are proud of what we can offer the world and proud of our standards of decency at work.

Eddie Izzard, patron of Hope not Hate:

'One of Britain's greatest strengths is its diversity. We are all descended from Angles, Saxons, Celts, Vikings and Romans and people from many other backgrounds have strengthened our national mix. Our society is stronger for being made up of lots of different genes, bloodlines, colours, skins and ideas.

Our diversity brings not just strength, but innovation, creativity and invention.

I've seen this in lots of different ways over the last decade. Through my work positively campaigning against racism and fascism with Hope not Hate, running across the UK for Sport Relief, and as an ambassador for the games makers at the London 2012 Olympics, where I saw British people of every background coming together to get behind Team GB.

One of the things that makes me proud about the Labour Party is that we embrace our country as it is – not just some old-fashioned idea of it. Our party stands for the people we see around us every day. For me, voting Labour is part of continuing that legacy of being on the right side of the moral and human argument, and of valuing freedom, dignity and tolerance above all else.'

A Labour vision of immigration

As Chuka Umunna sets out in his chapter, Labour believes in making markets work, and that free and unlimited markets don't work well. This is just as true for the labour market, and free movement of labour across Europe clearly has some downsides that we will address. There is nothing in Labour history, values or traditions that requires us to be in favour, in principle, of unlimited immigration. We are not, and never have been; we have and always will be for managed migration.

This means, the next time any more countries apply to join the EU, Labour will make sure that their citizens have to wait the maximum amount of time possible – currently a minimum of seven years

– before being able to come here to work. Labour will make learning English a priority for new arrivals, and prioritise English language teaching, rather than spending on translation services so that those who do come integrate and make our community stronger.

A Labour government in 2015 would make our community stronger by enforcing border control so that everyone who lives here is entitled to be here. What does that mean? It is the basic things that people expect – proper exit and entry checks and quickly removing those who have lost the right to stay. When people are here we need to make sure the rules are applied fairly in work, with access to homes, and in our public services.

Labour will enforce tough measures to ensure everyone is treated fairly. This includes cracking down on exploitation by gangmasters, rogue landlords, people smugglers and the modern-day slave trade. For example, Labour will:

- Enforce the national minimum wage, so unscrupulous bosses don't use migrants to undercut wages. Labour will increase the maximum fine for those attempting to pay below the national minimum wage to £50,000.
- Stop the appalling exploitation of people at work by gangmasters. That is why Labour set up the Gangmasters' Licensing Authority and it is why we will extend it to new areas like catering and tourism.
- Strengthen the law to make sure it is illegal for recruitment agencies just to recruit from abroad for jobs here at home.
- Improve the skills of our young people with new gold standard vocational qualifications and more high quality apprenticeships.
- Make sure we give people here the skills they need for the future by ensuring that companies bringing in workers from outside the EU also have to offer an apprenticeship.
- Take seriously the unfairness of people getting benefits but not contributing to the system. That is why Labour will work

to reform the welfare laws in Europe to stop child benefit going back to children who live elsewhere in Europe and why we will ensure you can't claim out of work benefits for at least six months after arriving in this country.

We also have to take action on those that help encourage illegal immigration to our shores. Too often there is a human price paid by some of those seeking safety or a better life in Britain, as we saw this summer when one man died in a container filled with thirty-five people (including children), discovered at Tilbury docks in Thurrock. Those who exploit such desperation should feel the full force of the law, and under a Labour government they would.

Managed immigration: the economic case

Britain would not be Britain without immigration. Our economy and the jobs it sustains would fail if we couldn't attract the best and the brightest to our country. UK society wouldn't be as rich without immigration. Anybody who says they will end immigration is not telling the truth. What they won't admit is that an end to immigration would be letting Britain down.

Our history as a nation is filled with examples of how people moving to this country has enriched and helped shape the success of our islands. Even now, there are very few people that don't want their football team to sign a star striker because he's Spanish, and most people don't refuse treatment if their NHS surgeon was born outside of Britain. Our businesses do better when they can trade with people across the world and when we can recruit people with the skills and attitude we need to be a successful and growing economy. Just look at Airbus in north Wales; it is the most successful business in the region that produces over half the world's aircraft and sustains 7,000 jobs in Flintshire alone. It relies on the cooperation and skills of French, German, Spanish and British workers.

That doesn't mean immigration never causes problems; as we've made clear we do need a sensible conversation about how to make immigration work for the UK and make sure the real concerns people have about it are addressed.

The British people are fair-minded: they will welcome people who come here legally to work and to enhance our economy and communities, who want to integrate into the UK, learn the language and will respect the UK's laws and customs.

There is no great clamour for overseas students, entrepreneurs and highly skilled migrants to be barred from coming to Britain, so it is a sign of just how incompetent this government is that David Cameron's key promise on immigration, their net migration target, treats all these immigration cases the same.

Indeed, the logic of the government's position is that they would celebrate if the number of young British people leaving to go and work abroad increased, while the number of foreign students coming to study at our universities reduced.

Under this government, companies expecting a quick turnaround on a simple visa are effectively being turned away, with business visas now taking over 50 per cent longer to process than they did in 2010, and the number receiving an initial response within the Home Office target of four weeks has fallen by 49 per cent.

Business demands better. Britain should not be turning away the best and the brightest because of a false promise. Under David Cameron and Theresa May the system is a mess, with illegal immigration getting worse, the backlog never ending and people increasingly thinking Britain is not open for study or business, which is bad for everyone.

If we want an economic recovery that works for everyone instead of just those at the top, we need to boost our economy and create jobs, and that means that the brightest and best people from across the world who want to invest in our country or learn skills to take back to their own nations should be welcome. They could be the CEOs and prime ministers of the future. Being welcoming to them while they study here is a long-term investment in the future of our country.

We don't want a race to the bottom in work and skills. Instead, under Labour, we will invest in the skills of our workforce, support our entrepreneurs and create the better-quality jobs with security and progress that give people pride and dignity in employment.

Fairness for all communities

It is not just jobs and the economy that are affected by immigration. Housing and a sense of community and belonging can be disrupted by rapid change. Nevertheless, thoughtful management of change can enhance a community's strength.

In some places, people have been able to find common threads that connect them to the people who have newly arrived. In many areas, for example, the arrival of Polish immigrants has meant Catholic churches are now full every Sunday. Part of Labour's vision is building communities from the ground up, and these sorts of shared experiences are a crucial part of doing just that.

And for those who say it can't or shouldn't be done by the state, look at what Labour has done in practice on a local level.

The common thread of a shared faith or culture is not always evident, so, for example, Labour-run Newham council offer English language lessons for free; this means that regardless of where you are from, there is no barrier to understanding the country in which you live.

In Thurrock, council homes are only available if you have lived in the borough for five years. This reassures residents that scant local resources are allocated to those who have shown a commitment to the community by living here for some time.

A 'local links' policy for housing like this is a basic way to establish Labour as a party that recognises that homes are about community as much as they are about a roof over your head. When people know about the policy, they like it, and it is welcomed by those who would previously have asked 'houses for whom?' when politicians talked about building more homes. It sends a message that investment is local first and foremost.

Labour's national commitment to building new homes is vital, but numbers on their own don't tell the story of what we want this country to be: homes built in communities with accessible public services, affordable for 'the many', including a variety of ways to get access, not limited to the narrow funnels of either the council waiting list or a massive deposit. Creating more opportunities to have your own place before you are thirty, and to keep a connection to your local area, near your job and your family, are what our plans are all about. Protecting everyone from slum landlords is why Newham has a register for private landlords, and Thurrock conducts 'health checks' on privately rented homes to tackle poor standards.

And let's be clear about the standards we need in our public services. In Thurrock, our Ockendon Studio School is specialising in customer service. In a community where retail dominates, this is sensible for ensuring our young people are fit for work, but also creates a culture of high standards where they can compete with the best.

It also means there will be no excuse for employers hiring people without basic skills like speaking English when caring for our older people, or dealing with tenants when refurbishing their homes. Labour is in the business of nation building; the idea that everyone in the UK has a responsibility to create a country that works is at the core of our identity.

Ruth Smeeth, Labour's prospective parliamentary candidate for Stoke North:

'In recent years the public debate over immigration has too often been emotionally charged and used by groups who seek to exploit people's fears for the future and damage community relations. Labour will never stoop to that level.

We need an open and honest debate that takes underlying concerns about immigration into account, rather than viewing migration in isolation. In Stoke-on-Trent, that includes an industrial strategy that brings high-skilled jobs to our community, investment in affordable housing and a real minimum wage.

Labour will address these anxieties by running a campaign grounded in hope and aspiration that offers a better future for all. That's the best way we can defeat the politics of fear at the ballot box and in our communities.'

Conclusion

For far too long this government has been about managing decline, resigned to the idea we are a lesser nation than we used to be, with no ambition for our future. UKIP are even more pessimistic about our role in the world and what we should be able to offer our citizens as a nation. Labour has a positive patriotic approach: ours is a great country and a growing one, for good reasons – we nurture and promote talent and hard work and it will be rewarded.

Tilbury in Thurrock has a glorious history as a place of defence, where Henry VIII built a fort to protect the realm and his daughter Elizabeth rallied the troops. More recently, it has been the gateway to the world: a port built mainly by Irish immigrants where global trade thrives and the harshness of change can blow cold on workers without protections.

It is where the *Windrush* docked and where cruise liners now drop off tourists bound for London. It is here where the past and the future, the anxieties and the pride of our great nation ebb and flow. It is here where an immigration policy has to work, for those with ambitions to succeed and be secure, for those born here and those who arrive.

Be in no doubt – Labour will have an approach to immigration that can make places like Thurrock and Delyn thrive just as well as our bustling cities. The modern world demands it and our values will show the way. The people who built this country came from all backgrounds and skills – the people who build the next generation will do so supported by the values of Labour.

Polly Billington is Labour's prospective parliamentary candidate for Thurrock, David Hanson is the Member of Parliament for Delyn and the shadow Minister for Immigration.

SECTION 3

A BETTER POLITICS

At a time when the British public feel deep disenchantment and distrust with Westminster, every party is talking about how to deliver better politics for the people of this country. But what better politics means depends on your values and your beliefs.

The whole point of democracy is that everyone should have an equal say, and Labour believes that the vote of a mum looking after her kids or someone who is unemployed is worth no less than the vote of a millionaire. But better politics is not just about elections.

Labour values are about creating a country in which everyone has a stake and where everyone should have an equal say and an equal opportunity. And that society is more prosperous when everyone has their chance to get on in life.

We don't want to see anyone held back by prejudice rooted in class, gender, ethnicity or sexual orientation. Our politics is about inclusion because we believe that is the right of every individual, but also important for the success of our economy. We don't want to see the growing gap between the 'haves' and the 'have-nots'. That's why we introduced the national minimum wage and are promoting a living wage. And we don't want basic rights – like health care – to depend on whether you can afford them, which is why we set up and have always backed the NHS.

When the Tories are in power you see a stark contrast with Labour values. Under the Tories, the NHS is always undermined and people find the services they depend on are under greater pressure. We're seeing that now with the NHS reorganisation that breeds fragmentation and means patients wait longer in A&E and to see the GP. The agenda to drive forward tackling inequality has stalled. Government rhetoric is no comfort when they have refused to implement key parts of the Equality Act.

Better politics means listening to people in all the regions of our country, in Scotland and Wales. It means devolution of power, not a top-down pulling of levers. We need that active and open politics, especially at a time when people think they are not being listened to or think that politicians don't understand their lives. That's why diversity in our politics is also important – Parliament must look and sound like the people it represents. So, while policies are important, so too is how we do our politics. And, as with everything else, Labour's politics is rooted in a belief in equality and the sharing of power for the greater good.

Harriet Harman QC MP is Labour's Deputy Leader.

Chapter 8

People-Led Politics

STELLA CREASY MP

'I remain just one thing, and one thing only, and that is a clown. It places me on a far higher plane than any politician.'

— Charlie Chaplin

Politics is about change and how best to achieve it. As a political movement, Labour campaigns for office not just to change government, but also to change lives. We cannot do that alone. The nature of the challenges facing us means it is only when each of us plays our part in addressing them – whether as citizens, consumers or campaigners – that we can truly overcome them in a way in which all can benefit.

That is why Britain's deepening disengagement from politics threatens our values and our vision for our shared future. When the public loses confidence in the belief we can harness our collective strengths to achieve outcomes for the good of ourselves and each other, the market becomes the default determinant of the results achieved. Restoring faith in collective action is more than a requirement for winning elections, it is the very lifeblood of our politics.

It is for this reason our plans to empower the public go well beyond constitutional and electoral reform – vital though Labour believes such measures to be. Our mission is nothing less than to put the power to rebuild Britain firmly in the grasp of the people.

If voting changed anything...

Make no mistake, of course how the public vote in elections matters to Labour: winning office is critical to our ability to put into practice the policies and proposals we have for a better Britain. However, sometimes it can seem as if the only role we ask of the public is to elect Labour, that who runs the government is all that matters, and all we ask from activists and individuals is simply to go to the ballot box and then pay the tax bill at the end.

This reflects the domination of the belief that centrally organised and managed services are the best way to tackle inequality. We know an individual can only make limited choices – no matter how wealthy they are – but together we can decide to create not just different lives, but a different world. At its best, the history of the Labour movement reflects how the promise of collective action can be translated into practical outcomes – from collaborating to build a National Health Service to fighting for equalities legislation and a national minimum wage – of which we are rightly proud. In doing so, Labour has shown time and time again the difference working collectively can make to every generation.

A focus on institutions as a vehicle for collective action may make sense in economic models or political theory textbooks, but the experience of the difficulties of actually achieving social change shows it requires a multitude of responses. Whether addressing climate change, social mobility, public health, national security or economic growth, the messy reality of inequality means legislation alone is rarely enough.

Alternative models of service provision rooted in mutualism and cooperatives have also always been part of Labour's history. However, recognition of how working in these ways to empower the public is vital – not just to gain their support for services but in the outcomes achieved – has only come to the fore in recent years. Faced with sometimes seemingly impossible issues, we know our best hope comes from building networks where individuals and communities, as well as private and public bodies both at home and internationally, are able and willing to act.

If we leave uncontested the idea that all political movements are the same, then the primary forces that will shape our world will be the loudest voices or the largest wallets. As progressives we are therefore concerned about the nature of our political culture, not just because it makes people less likely to vote – and so support our candidates – but because it drains the power of collective action from Britain.

Just how bad is it?

Declining participation in the formal political process has been a feature of our political landscape for decades. In the '50s turnout was around eight out of ten people, it fell to 59 per cent in 2001 and has now risen back to 65 per cent in 2010. Ahead of the next election, the numbers of people saying they will definitely vote has consistently polled at around 58 per cent, although the Hansard Society Audit of Political Engagement highlights how among certain groups – young people in particular – these figures are much lower.

While most professions have suffered a decline in trust over recent history, politicians have fared especially badly. Research shows even those who do vote now don't trust the motivations of politicians. In 2013, a third of the public said that they 'almost never' trust 'British governments of any party to place the needs of the nation above the interests of their own political party' – three times as many as took this view in 1986. At the same time, the proportion that trust the government 'just about always' or 'most of the time' has more than halved (17 per cent in 2013, down from 38 per cent in 1986).

A lack of trust in politicians while still on the whole voting for them would be one thing, but there is now growing evidence that more and more of the public don't think politicians can actually make a difference even if they could be believed. Hansard's work shows that an increasing number of the public are ambivalent about politics itself. While 63 per cent of the public say that if they are dissatisfied with political decisions they have a duty to do something about it, only half have undertaken any form of political activism. Fewer than one in ten people have created or signed a petition either on or offline and only 8 per cent have contacted an elected representative. In total only 32 per cent believe that if people 'like me' get involved, they can change the way the country is run. Instead, their attention is turning to community campaigns or simply tuning out altogether.

For modern Britain, politics isn't just full of those you think you cannot trust. It is increasingly considered less and less relevant as a mechanism for social change. This perception comes at the same time as when achieving our goals requires even more people to give both their vote and their voice to progressive activism. Rebuilding the relationship between the public and the body politic is not simply good for our democracy, it is imperative for our future ambitions.

Labour's Policy Review: power for the people

It is for this reason Labour's Policy Review has focused on devolving power. That means asking across every area how to reconfigure the way our country works so that the public themselves are given the tools, time and resources they need to take control of their own lives as well as collaborate with others for mutual benefit.

What then does this mean in practice? Certainly electoral and constitutional reform is key. We know we need to make Parliament more relevant and broader in its work as well as more accessible; these challenges range from how people are voted in to how they can engage in the debates, discussions and decisions it takes. Our plans extend well beyond resolving the future of the House of Lords and reforming how our electoral system works. Labour is also committed to remodelling the democratic process so the public can more easily understand and engage with the making of laws. This includes new methods for the public to participate in the scrutiny and production of legislation itself, including the way in which draft bills and public reading stages of laws are managed.

Starting early is also vital, as Bex Bailey has set out in her chapter. We now face a generation that is active within social campaigns and sees politics primarily as a sidebar issue – a distraction from campaigning at best and a cesspit of corruption and broken promises at worst. Labour will ensure citizenship is a key part of our national curriculum, with teachers given the training and time to develop the civic interest of every young person in Britain. Such an approach won't stop at the school gates: working in partnership with voluntary and community organisations young people will be given more opportunities throughout their lives to volunteer as well as participate in civil society. As part of this, extending the franchise to all those aged sixteen is key to honouring the contribution they make to our country. This is a new contract with Britain's future, the young people upon whose ideas and energy our national success depends.

Gloria De Piero MP, shadow Minister for Women and Equalities:

'A politics that doesn't look or sound like Britain won't represent Britain.

Today, three-quarters of the Cabinet are men, and there are still more male MPs today than there have ever been women elected to Parliament. It took Labour to pioneer all-women shortlists and flood Parliament with more women and I am proud that 44 per cent of Labour's shadow Cabinet are now women.

We will continue to lead on making our politics more representative, but the other parties must start pulling their weight. More than half of our candidates in target seats are women, compared to 77 per cent of Tory target seat candidates being men.

What ultimately matters to women across the country though is not just who holds the power, but what decisions you take. Just as the government has shut women's voices out, it has hit women hardest. One in four working women is now earning less than the living wage, record numbers of women are self-employed earning less than the minimum wage, and the pay gap is back on the rise after years of progress under Labour.

Just as it will take Labour to deliver a more representative politics, it will take a Labour government to deliver a better future for women and their families.'

Sadiq Khan MP, shadow Justice Secretary and co-chair of Labour's Race Equality Consultation:

'Public institutions must properly represent our wonderfully diverse country. From politics and the judiciary to the police, representative institutions are more effective and engender higher public confidence.

Labour elected the first ethnic minority MPs in modern times, and appointed Paul Boateng as the first minority ethnic Cabinet member in 2002. From the Race Equality Act to the Stephen Lawrence Inquiry, it is a track record we should be immensely proud of.

Our public institutions, however, remain hugely unrepresentative and increasing diversity will be a top priority for Ed Miliband's government. We will embed a race equality strategy at the heart of government. We will change the law so the police can pursue proactive employment strategies. We will increase the number of ethnic minority senior civil servants to at least 8 per cent by 2020. We will appoint more ethnic minority and women judges and the private sector is on notice that we will legislate if they don't improve the diversity of company boards voluntarily.

Together, this constitutes the most radical plan to improve diversity and tackle racial discrimination from any opposition, ever.'

Community organisation

The importance of reviving mass participation in politics goes beyond our concerns for the responsiveness of Britain's formal decision-making processes. It is also about how ideas and debates are developed in the first place. Our understanding of how people can express opinions is, at present, dominated by the notion that it involves conflict, with winners and losers being the end result. This is because our experience of how people can have their say is still too shaped by the belief that the only time in which anyone exercises influence is in an election. Most of the tools we know to express opinions and debate, whether on or offline, tend towards critique alone; petitions, lobbies and demonstrations should be but one element of a vibrant political sphere rather than its dominant features. If we want a world in which we seek answers and action as well as offering analysis and anger, then we also need tools to help find consensus on next steps too.

Community organising offers techniques that encourage us to ask what we have in common and how can we work together to achieve it, seeking relationships that will endure, not just easy wins that can sometimes alienate. This will help us bridge the gap between the important roles social campaigns can play in challenging established thinking and the need for political movements that can take action. It is these lessons of relational politics that organisations like the Movement for Change are bringing to Labour's work.

The track record of those working in this way to secure progressive outcomes – from tackling legal loan-sharking, safety measures for women and housing access – as well as inspiring individuals into participation and local leadership, is impressive. In developing opportunities to work in this way in the years ahead, Labour is determined to unlock the time, effort and energy of activists so that they can be catalysts of change in their communities.

Mike Kane, Member of Parliament for Wythenshawe & Sale East and former CEO of Movement for Change:

'The Labour movement has always worked hard throughout our history to bring more ordinary people into public life. This tradition is alive and well in our politics today, with many activists across the country using community organising techniques to make a difference in our neighbourhoods.

One recent example from my constituency was when the local Labour Party branch kept getting feedback about problems caused by derelict buildings. They took action by building relationships with other groups in their village and brought 120 people together to demonstrate and call for change, forcing the main landlord to act. It sums up Labour's aspiration of not only winning elections, but doing politics in a better way. Community organising can help us achieve that.'

Cllr Steve Doran, Dartford Borough Council:

'I used to be sceptical about whether politics had anything to offer for someone like me. That changed when I attended an event about tackling legal loan sharks and told the room about my own struggle with payday lenders.

It was the first time I'd admitted my poor financial planning skills in public and I was shocked by the response. I wasn't immediately ejected from the room. I wasn't ignored. I was listened to and invited to get involved a campaign that would force the government to cap the cost of credit.

Working with Movement for Change has given me new skills, more confidence and taught me that I'm not valuable in spite of my unfortunate experiences; I am all the more valuable because of my experiences. Now I'm a Labour councillor, having won my election by one vote. It just shows the difference that each one of us can make.'

Labour's operating system: accountability v. participation

Our commitment to empowering the British people is threaded throughout our intention not simply to devolve power to local communities but also beyond, to the public themselves. We know, however, that sometimes local government structures can be as exclusive as national ones.

That is why, as my colleague Steve Reed addresses in his chapter, Labour is determined not just to give the public more say over their services but more direct control over them too. Existing institutions and practices at both a local and national level can all too often drain rather than energise public engagement.

Countless rounds of meetings and minutes with individuals who are there to explain decisions already made can sometimes turn participation into an Olympian effort only the few can endure. In a time-poor society many underestimate just what a barrier these ways of working can be both to those who want to take part, and the ability of those who do to make constructive progress.

Modern communication can offer some ways of short-circuiting these problems; certainly social media and online networks offer new ways to bring more diverse groups of people together and balance home and work commitments. However, transferring meetings online doesn't make them any less onerous or empowering. The evidence of the difficulties one in five people has with basic online tasks, and that this is overwhelmingly among those from lower socio-economic backgrounds, also means we should be wary of presuming there is a technical fix alone which can make participation easy and worthwhile for all of Britain.

Creating a culture of relational politics means being clear about what impact any involvement has on outcomes. Labour will draw careful distinction between opportunities to hold representatives to account for the decisions they have made, and direct participation in either the design or delivery of change. Too often these can get confused, with claims made that methods of accountability – such as meetings with councillors or officials – are the same as participation.

The limited success of many previous attempts at engagement have been in part due to a lack of clarity about what real power those who take part have, leaving those who do engage confused and frustrated. It is a mistake the present government continues to make. Whether their approach to public involvement in policing, healthcare or schools, their plans offer more meetings but little real influence to victims, patients, parents or pupils.

We know a poor experience of involvement is worse than no involvement at all in motivating people to take part. Political elites have sometimes acted as though the public cannot cope with difficult choices or understand complexity, holding consultations after decisions have been made to secure consent, rather than recognising the greater gains in cooperation to be had if the public are given ownership of their own futures. Labour's approach to reform of public services seeks to challenge that culture, not just giving the public a greater say, but a greater direct responsibility for the outcomes achieved.

Exercising power isn't about being in the room with those who make decisions about you, but helping to make decisions yourself. That is why our approach is rooted in recognition that real power for the people is not simply about offering more meetings or even more reports. Instead, Labour will give more direct control – of money, service priorities and outcomes – to those who use services both individually and collectively.

Whether extending the use of personal care payments, supporting mutual models of service delivery or devolving decision-making to regions, we know user involvement can not only improve value for money, it can also improve outcomes. Those who decry 'the usual suspects' as a cover for not devolving more decision-making and participation opportunities to the public miss the point. That only some participate highlights that we need to change the method of participation to one in which more people wish to undertake, rather than blaming those who do show up.

Building this new culture of empowerment and engagement won't come easy. Traditionally the left has always been better at fighting for services for people rather than working with them. But shaking off the tendency to view inequality as something that can only be tackled by central institutions is key to our offer to the British public at the next election. This is our new operating system for social justice. Labour will put the people of Britain firmly in the driving seat for our nation's future – ours will be a politics not for the people, but with them.

Stella Creasy is the Member of Parliament for Walthamstow and the shadow Minister for Competition and Consumer Affairs.

Chapter 9

People-Powered Public Services

STEVE REED MP

'This devolution of power is the right thing to do for the users of public services and is the right way to show that we can do more with less.'
— Ed Miliband MP, Leader of the Labour Party, Hugo Young Lecture, February 2014

Public services were set up to create a fairer society. They offer help when people need it, collectively provide the things that people on their own cannot obtain, and give people the opportunity to lead more successful lives. That is why we have a National Health Service, state schools, public housing, unemployment benefits, and care services for older and disabled people.

Their purpose is social justice, an objective central to Labour's values. The problem we face as a society is that we've lost some focus on the outcome because we've got stuck defending the processes used in the past to try and deliver it. As the country deals with the consequences of the global banking crisis with less money available to spend, it is striking how often we hear people talk about defending services rather than defending the outcomes those services are trying to achieve. The problem with confusing means with ends is we miss the opportunity of finding different ways of doing things that might have other benefits besides costing less.

Labour councils have already realised this as they try to protect people from becoming the victims of government funding cuts. Labour's Policy Review is learning from this experience and putting the reform of public services centre-stage. The common principle that runs right through Labour's new approach is empowerment. Ed Miliband pledged in his Hugo Young Memorial Lecture earlier this year that a commitment to people-powered public services would be at the heart of the next Labour government's mission. By handing power to people who don't have it we can help them transform lives, communities, politics and public services.

Power to the people

The Blenheim Gardens council housing estate in Brixton was for years a place people wanted to get out of. It had high levels of crime including anti-social behaviour, drug dealing and prostitution. Basic housing services like repairs, lighting and cleaning were substandard. Rent collection rates were low. Today it is a place transformed. With the full support of their Labour council, residents took control through an elected residents' management board which took responsibility for the housing managers, staff and the estate budget.

Repairs are now at a much higher standard than other estates. The estate is visibly cleaner, rent collection rates are high, crime is lower, anti-social behaviour has been reduced, and the estate is so efficiently run that they were able to generate savings, which they used to turn the mall, a previously run-down tarmac space in the middle of the estate, into an attractive and well-maintained garden. All this happened because the staff who run the estate had to answer directly to the residents instead of to managers and politicians in the town hall. The residents used their power to transform their neighbourhood with higher quality services that cost less.

Eamon Maguire, tenant of the Blenheim Gardens Housing Estate, Brixton:

'I've experienced the difference between an estate directly managed by the council with no input from residents and one that is overseen by an elected residents' management board insisting on better standards of service. When the short-life housing cooperative that I was a member of was wound up by the local authority in 2009, we were given high priority on the housing list and were required to bid for anything suitable.

My first viewing was of a property directly let by Lambeth. I arrived punctually for the viewing but the officer conducting the viewing did not. I waited in communal areas that were seedy and unattractive. When the officer did arrive he was very high-handed and offered no explanation for his lateness. He could offer no information about the estate itself and very little about the property, such as its repair history or proposed improvements.

I was offered the property but requested twenty-four hours to decide. When I called up with my decision, the officer was unavailable and no one else seemed to know anything about the issue. Not surprisingly, I declined the property.

My experience was very different when I viewed a property on the Blenheim Gardens Estate, which was far more pleasant and well kept. The viewing commenced promptly and the estate's maintenance manager was unfailingly polite, friendly and candid. He was very informed about the estate and was able to offer a number of options for small alterations that could be made to the property in future to meet my requirements.

Making the people who run public services directly accountable to those who use them works.'

Preventing problems and strengthening partnerships

Too many of our existing public services deal with failure rather than preventing failure from happening in the first place. Barnardo's points out that the children of prisoners are three times more likely than other children to become offenders themselves, so why don't we do more to stop that happening? Prisoners' families need support to cope with the consequences of having a parent removed from the home, or other problems such as drug dependency, financial instability or exposure to violence or abuse at an earlier age that may have contributed to the parent's offending.

If you speak to people living in neighbourhoods with high levels of crime, they will tell you they'd rather see action to stop people offending than deal with the after effects later on. That is not only rational, but it costs far less too. The stark fact that 70 per cent of young offenders reoffend within twelve months of being released from custody tells us that locking up young criminals, on its own, is not enough. It costs more to lock up a young offender for a year than to send a child to Eton, but the money is doing little to stop young people committing crime or help them become useful members of society.

Tackling problems at source can seem more difficult than dealing with the after effects later on. Effective early intervention in complex families requires different public services to work together instead of each doing their own thing in isolation. Social workers, health professionals, probation and police officers, housing managers and many others need to work in a much closer partnership centred on the needs and challenges of the family they are trying to support. It is important that the family or offender is able to help take the decisions that will affect them. This ensures that their own experience is brought to bear in solving the problems, and also helps them rebuild a sense of self-reliance that may be lacking.

Junior Smart, ex-offender, now Business Relationships Manager at St Giles Trust:

'Young people caught up in gangs are very hard to reach. They have chaotic backgrounds, do not trust anyone they perceive as being an authority figure, and have difficulty engaging with services which are intended to support them.

This is why the St Giles Trust's SOS Project takes a grassroots approach. We use trained, reformed ex-offenders to provide support for the clients we are trying to reach. Having 'walked in the same shoes' as their clients, they have a level of authenticity and credibility which statutory support services are unable to achieve. They are living proof that change is possible and become inspirational role models.

SOS is highly effective at changing ex-offenders' thinking and behaviour. We work with around 400 young offenders with the highest risk of re-offending across London each year. An evaluation this year found that 87 per cent of our clients had changed their attitudes towards offending. The small amount of money spent on each client saves vast amounts more by preventing future offending with all its associated social and financial costs.'

The importance of people's social networks

Public services tend to see people as problems rather than opportunities and deal with them as if their own relationships and networks do not matter very much. Backr is a project run by the social enterprise Participle that helps unemployed people find work by strengthening the social networks they are part of. It is a radically different approach from the Tory-led government's failing Work Programme, and is far more effective.

First of all, Backr recognises that over half of all job vacancies are never formally advertised; they're filled, instead, by word of mouth. If you're not part of the network of people who are talking to each other about these vacancies, you'll never find out about them. So, Backr brings people from in-work networks and connects them with people who are outside them, building connections through people. Backr then trains up people who already have jobs to coach people looking for work by offering friendly advice and support. Unemployed people are more likely to find out about job vacancies and find the support they need to try and get them.

This is a much more effective way of helping people back into long-term employment than repeatedly sending them on pointless CV writing courses or making them work for nothing doing things they have no interest in. It is a much more human-centred approach than making people sit in front of a desk facing an anonymous civil servant in a job centre. Instead of seeing themselves as the public services see them – a problem because they are unemployed – this more relational, personalised approach helps unemployed people to regain their self-confidence.

New technology creates new ways for people to engage with each other and with the people who run the services they use. This creates a new relational model of public services with much more public scrutiny, sharing of experiences, and participation in decision-making than was ever possible before.

Backr Case Study: a relational approach to finding work:

Twenty-year-old Rob Jeffrey, who lives in Durham, was on an IT apprenticeship at a secondary school. He studied graphic design at college and enrolled on a university degree course in game design. Ultimately, he wasn't able to complete the course and signed up to Backr to look for work opportunities and build some new contacts.

Searching Backr's website, Rob found a graphic design opportunity posted by a young businesswoman who was working with Backr as a coach. He'd been pursuing graphic design as a hobby but his lack of formal qualifications kept holding him back. Backr's informal approach made it easier to use than more traditional ways of finding jobs. Rob was able to make a very personal approach, tell his story how he wanted, and he secured some short-term project work as a result.

The project gave Rob invaluable experience of working with clients, practising communication styles and learning the kinds of questions to ask. He has now set up his own business in graphic design, Redchevron, and is excited about building it.

In Rob's own words: 'If I hadn't joined Backr I wouldn't have had the confidence in my ability or seen the potential to start my own business. It was the pick-me-up that I needed. I really got to showcase myself as a person.'

Power, prevention, partnerships and people

We can learn lessons from these three examples that are relevant to public services and politics more widely.

First, making public services directly accountable to the people who use them makes them more effective and more responsive.

Second, people living with a problem would rather the problem was prevented from happening than managed afterwards.

Third, we need stronger partnerships of people with different professional expertise that are centred on and involve the individual or group they are trying to help.

Fourth, bringing people together and recognising the importance of their own relationships, instead of dealing with people's problems in isolation, gives you a better chance of resolving them.

Learning to let go

Extending this people-powered approach right across public services presents huge challenges. For politicians and senior service managers it means letting go of our power to take all the decisions. Sir Steve Houghton cites in his chapter how difficult this has proved for David Cameron's government. It also means admitting that, on our own, politicians don't have all the answers. This is very unnatural behaviour for politicians who, in the past, have encouraged a parent–child relationship where they claim to know what's best for people. Instead we need an adult–adult relationship where we share information, power and decision-making to meet the challenges we face.

Once we let go, we will find that different communities try different approaches. That presents another challenge since along with more innovation comes the risk that some things may go wrong. The point about mistakes is not whether they're made but whether we learn from them. The current way we run things leads to frequent mistakes but we keep repeating them. If politicians try to eliminate risk by imposing a uniform one-size-fits-all approach everywhere then we will stifle innovation and continue to maintain the self-defeating pretence that politicians in Whitehall can control everything.

Rebuilding trust

Trust in politics is at an all-time low, as many of the other authors in this book have pointed out. The expenses scandal crystallised a long-held fear that politicians were in it for themselves. That, together with the banking crisis, global financial crash and recession that followed, and the hacking scandal in the media, has shaken the pillars upon which our democracy rests. Nevertheless, as Dan alluded to in his introduction, the breakdown in trust didn't start with the crash in 2008 – the problem runs much deeper.

Labour understands that we will not win back people's trust in politicians until politicians learn to trust the people. We need a more adult politics where information is open and shared and the real challenges laid bare. We need a more adult approach to decision-making in the public services where power is shared with the people whose lives it affects.

The current Tory-led government has completely failed to understand this and gave up on serious reform almost as soon as they were elected. Their Big Society idea quickly shrivelled into an attempt to replace public service professionals with cheaper volunteers. What they call 'localism' is really about Tory ministers in Whitehall telling people what to do locally. The Tories refuse to understand that the key to improving public services is making the professionals directly accountable to the people they serve and sharing decision-making power with the people those decisions affect.

Lisa Nandy MP, shadow Minister for Civil Society:

'The Big Society got some things right. It recognised that while politicians spend time arguing about the state and the market, we too often neglect communities. Society is where some of our greatest assets – kindness, respect, energy, creativity – lie. But David Cameron ignored the fact that across the country too many families lack the time, resources, confidence or opportunities to play their part. The Conservative idea that if government pulls back communities will thrive left some parts of Britain to sink while others swim.

Labour understands that government has to be a partner, walking alongside people on this journey to a fairer, stronger society. We will act to break up concentrations of power, so that we all have an equal voice, create responsive, flexible public services and ensure people have decent pay, housing and childcare so they can take part. It's only Labour that can do this, empower people and strengthen communities because it is in our DNA, a party that was built from the grassroots, ordinary people standing up for themselves and for others to build a better Britain.'

A grassroots state

Labour in local government is already showing how different the next Labour government will be, as Steve Houghton outlines in his chapter. Rochdale has mutualised their entire council housing stock to give residents power over how their homes are managed. Edinburgh is piloting a city-wide childcare scheme that gives people more control over the kind of childcare they want, while making it more affordable. Oldham is giving unemployed people a bigger say over what support or training they need to get back into work, rather than sending them on prescriptive and unsuccessful government courses. Plymouth is setting up community energy projects based on a partnership between the council and the community to generate energy sustainably and reduce household bills.

However, a national political programme based on shifting power to the people requires more than a series of separate initiatives. It requires a wholesale reshaping of the relationship between citizens and the state, and a bold, clear vision of what that relationship needs to be in the future.

Fundamentally, we must move from a top-down model of the state that does things *to* you towards a grassroots state that does things *with* you. The state must become an enabler, a facilitator, and stop trying to control everything.

Involving people more allows us to harness the insights and creativity of those who use public services to drive greater efficiency, or even to rethink the outcomes we're trying to achieve. That is how tenant-led housing estates like Blenheim Gardens have improved so dramatically. The state, in this case the local council, has empowered residents to direct how their homes are managed.

As Liz Kendall expands on in her chapter on living longer and healthier lives, there are big lessons from handing older and disabled people the power to choose how a budget allocated to them is spent. Some of them choose things that are radically different from what public services would have allocated to them. Instead of a few hours once a week in a day-care centre, they might choose instead to buy a caravan they can stay in with family or friends whenever they like. It costs the same, but it is not what the state would have provided.

As long as the service user ends up happier, why shouldn't we give them the choice? Personalised budgets of this kind become even more powerful if we support budget-holders to pool them to pay for things they want. That would give people more purchasing power to force change from service providers and move away from the atomisation and sense of isolation that some people with personalised care budgets dislike.

Labour understands that a 'take-it-or-leave-it' approach to public services is no longer enough. People lead lives that are unimaginably more varied than they were when our current model of public services was established after the Second World War. We choose the goods and services we want to consume and the lifestyle we want to live. Deference has been replaced by assertive individualism, and our country is a vibrant multi-ethnic and multicultural kaleidoscope. Public services will not survive unless they learn to adapt to the needs and expectations of different users. The only way to deal with complexity on that scale is to engage individuals and communities directly in helping to reshape the services they use. No centralised top-down model would be capable of doing that alone.

Many people who rely heavily on public services find, over time, or even over several generations, that they become so dependent on decisions taken about them by others that they lose the ability to aspire to anything different. By taking all the key decisions for them we take away people's self-reliance and their ability to dream bigger dreams. This is how welfare dependency is created, and the solution is to involve people in taking decisions about what they want to achieve and how they want to achieve it.

Building their capacity to participate may take time, but it is a necessary investment if we want to give people the power they need to take back control. The Tories completely misunderstand this. For them, dependency is based on the availability of benefits and their solution is to cut them. First, they make vulnerable people dependent on decisions taken by others, then they punish them for it by plunging them more deeply into poverty. While the Tories encourage a race to the bottom, Labour can use the politics of empowerment to help people lift themselves up.

If we're serious about handing people more power, government itself needs to change. Culture change must be accompanied by structural change. National government has a right to set the outcomes it wants as part of a negotiated deal involving a pooled funding pot, but it should then leave it to local government and communities to deliver the outcomes in the way that best suits their locality.

Labour's proposals for city-regions will create regional powerhouses outside London to which some strategic powers can be devolved. But councils must adapt too. Lambeth has reduced the council's ability to hoard power by abolishing powerful directorates and is developing new models of decision-making and accountability that give citizens, communities and front-line staff more control. This affects services as varied as youth services, town planning, housing and social care. They are developing a model of commissioning services that shares decision-making with service users, ensuring that people's real needs are what drive decisions and that services remain flexible and adaptable.

Case Study: Community-led regeneration
Deborah Bestwick, Director of Ovalhouse Theatre:

'The Ovalhouse Theatre is a radical community-based theatre in south London. After a number of false starts over recent years we are now moving premises as part of a new community-led regeneration called Future Brixton.

Lambeth's Labour Council, working with Ovalhouse, is financing the development of almost 300 affordable homes with 40 per cent at council rent levels, community and health facilities, a shop, social enterprise and training opportunities for young people, all right on the street in front of a new Ovalhouse theatre.

All of the ideas came from the community itself as part of a people-led approach. This makes for a very different regeneration project than the traditional developer-led model financed by private house sales. We maintain a relationship with the local community that suits Ovalhouse's brand and values and also means the community's own aspirations are at the heart of the whole project.'

The politics of empowerment

One Nation Labour is all about bridging the divides of wealth, opportunity and power that exist in our country. By harnessing the insights, experience and creativity of our own communities we can transform public services and deliver social justice even at a time of austerity. Doing that requires a revolution in our public services based on handing more power to the people.

People, not organisations that provide services, must be at the heart of everything public services do. Instead of being primarily decision-makers, politicians and political parties will become enablers who bring people together and link them to the resources they need to make the changes they want to see. The litmus test for whether we're getting it right is whether people feel they have more or less control over their own lives as a result. The politics of empowerment is already proving its worth in local government and is being demonstrated by community organisations up and down the country. If you vote Labour for people-powered public services, we will do something that no political party has done before: win power so that we can give it away.

Steve Reed is the Member of Parliament for Croydon North, a shadow Home Office Minister and a former Leader of Lambeth Council.

Chapter 10

A Local Future

SIR STEVE HOUGHTON

'An open democracy, in which government is held to account by the people, decisions are taken as far as practicable by the communities they affect…'
— Clause IV, Labour Party Constitution

It has been said that all politics is local. As someone who has worked in local government for more than twenty-five years, I know how important it is in shaping a community's faith in politics. Equally, I am convinced that reform of local public services is essential if we are to serve the public well at a time when austerity means we will have fewer resources, and when the public's aspirations and needs are changing significantly.

My experience as a Council Leader and as a member of the Local Government Association Executive tells me that the closer we can bring decision-making to people, the better the outcomes of those decisions are likely to be.

Having worked with the last Labour government on tackling long-term unemployment through partnership, working and inspiring the introduction of the Future Jobs Fund, I also know that decision-making needs to go beyond local councils if it is to be successful. Public engagement must reach across the public services and directly into communities themselves. It is the only way we will meet the challenges that lie ahead and restore faith in the political process.

That is why the next Labour government's approach will be a localist approach. We will shift power to the people on the front line – the reformers and innovators best placed to deliver better community services.

The financial, social and political challenges our country faces have local consequences that the centralised 'big power' of the state is not best placed to solve. Building solutions locally will also form a key part of responding to the constraints of austerity and managing demand in an already stretched system.

While all the main political parties have claimed to adopt localism in theory, only Labour is committed to it in practice. Labour councils across the country are already leading the way in this approach: opening up new opportunities; enabling participation in local democracy; and creating good places to live.

The term 'localism' is open to interpretation, however, and two very different approaches to it are emerging. The next general election will provide a real choice to the electorate on how they would like public services to be delivered in their community and what role they would like to play within them.

The Tory-led government's approach

David Cameron's commitment to localism over the last four years has been based more in rhetoric than reality. His government has pursued an ideological approach to local government and its services driven by their enthusiasm for a 'small state' that has resulted in significant powers being centralised to Whitehall.

Rather than spreading actual power, Tory localism has sought only to devolve responsibility and political blame for a fragmentation of local services and a funding settlement that has hit the poorest communities hardest.

It has two major features. The first is the approach to funding.

Local government has had to endure an average 33 per cent real terms cut since 2010, with a further 10 per cent reduction to come in the next spending round. This culminated in the Local Government Association's famous 'graph of doom'. It forecasts a funding cliff-edge and severe financial problems for once grant-dependent councils after 2018 as cost pressures on services go up and incomes come down.

The government's response has been to increasingly allow councils to retain their own incomes – principally business rates and council tax – therefore incentivising economic growth and reducing their dependency on central government grants. The problem is that the government has done this at the same time as penalising the most deprived areas through its overall funding settlement.

Any benefits of business rate retention have been dampened by an unfair approach to local funding that sees the areas that can afford it least being hit the hardest. The ten most deprived local authorities in England will lose sixteen times more in spending per head of population than the ten least deprived authorities. Hampshire's Hart District Council and Wokingham Borough Council – the two least deprived local authorities – are each losing £28 and £20 per head, respectively. By contrast, Liverpool and Hackney Councils' residents – the most in need – are losing £807 and £974 per head.[35] The overall result has been a redistribution of resources from poorer to more prosperous places, pushing some councils closer to the cliff-edge.

The second strand of government policy has been the changes enacted by the Localism Act, which claimed to give communities more say over service delivery. But while giving a general power of competence to councils, the act did not devolve power away from the centre. In fact, it gave the Secretary of State 126 new powers over local government. And while Eric Pickles has pretended to devolve with one hand, he has reduced the power of councils with the other – such as

---

35 *Mirror*, 'Poorest areas in Britain hit 16 times harder by budget cuts than richest areas', 25 August 2014.

his weakening of the planning laws, making it harder for communities to control the number of betting shops and payday lenders popping up on our high streets.

This squeeze from the centre has left the future role of councils and councillors in some doubt. Indeed, ministers have raised the issue of councillors being no more than well-intended 'volunteers' in future.

It is true to say ministers have been looking to devolve some funding and decision-making on the economy to Combined Authorities and Local Enterprise Partnerships, but, to date, progress has been slow and bureaucratic. So far, little has been achieved.

Ministers have instead sought to steer local decision-making on issues as diverse as rubbish collection to car parking rules. This is a government that clearly has little appetite for 'letting go'.

Consequently, 'localism' on David Cameron's watch has become little more than passing the buck to councils to decide which services to cut and when. It is now abundantly clear that if local government and local democracy are to survive and effectively serve people in future, then an alternative approach is needed.

A new approach

For localism to work there needs to be devolution in the political system at all levels.

The experience of piloting community budgets showed that savings can be made and service performance can be improved if decisions are made closer to and involve those affected by them and by greater multi-agency collaboration on the ground.

There are three key principles that should underpin a new localist model, namely:

- More power to people to shape services in response to their specific needs and those of their communities, and to become active citizens.

- Collaboration and cooperation between public services and organisations to stop inefficient duplication.
- Investment, early intervention and promotion of independence to avoid the costs of failure (prevention).

These principles have already been adopted by many Labour councils. Both Greater Manchester (Combined Authority) and Derbyshire (Two Tier) Councils for example have shown how collaboration with local delivery can work effectively on areas such as housing, health and social care integration and early years. Any new localist model, therefore, can build upon existing good practice as well as academic theory.

Any new model, of course, needs to be underpinned by a 'fair' system of resource distribution. Fair funding would not solve the problem of austerity but would at least ensure the issue of 'needs' is recognised, and give a much more level platform for a localist model to be based upon.

Labour is committed to revising resource allocation, recognising 'needs' alongside the desire to incentivise places to innovate and create economic growth. Without it, localism for the most vulnerable in society will remain a hollow promise.

That commitment shows a difference between a Labour approach to support the many, and the government's approach to encourage the few. The choice for people at the next election could not be clearer.

Hilary Benn MP, shadow Secretary of State for Communities and Local Government:

'You only have to think about our National Health Service and education for all children to be reminded of the power of politics to transform lives, and yet some have lost confidence in it. By passing power down to communities, we can restore confidence in its ability to change things for the better.

Labour's commitment to devolve power – to towns and cities, counties and districts – will help to change that. With less money about, we must make best use of what we have to create jobs, invest in transport and skills, encourage new businesses, build homes for families and provide support that stops problems arising in the first place rather than having to fix them expensively later on.

These are all good reasons to vote Labour, but it's what we do with devolved power that really matters. Each of us has a responsibility to contribute – we get out what we put in – and that's the kind of politics I believe in.'

Labour – making localism a reality

The next Labour government has a real opportunity to learn the lessons of the Tory-led government's failure on localism and to build upon the good practice already on the ground.

To do that, both central and local government politicians will need to share the levers of power if the three principles mentioned earlier are to be achieved.

As part of Labour's Policy Review, The Local Government Innovation Taskforce has been looking at what people-powered services could be, and its recommendations are both challenging and exciting.

A Labour government will offer a new deal to all English councils on issues which matter most to people, bringing about the biggest decentralisation of power in 100 years.

We would devolve central funding and decision-making in five key areas:

- Providing people with the care they need to live independently.
- Giving every young person the opportunity to get a decent job.
- Increasing community safety and reducing crime.
- Helping excluded families to overcome their challenges for good.
- Giving every child a good start in life.

Many Labour councils have been leading the way in these areas, providing ample evidence of what can be achieved.

Providing people with the care they need to live independently.

Greenwich Council's Integrated Care Partnership has created six integrated teams between Health and Social Care. As a result, 50 per cent less people now enter full health and social care pathways and the number of people being admitted to hospital has fallen by more than a quarter, saving £900,000 from the social care budget.

Giving every young person the opportunity to get a decent job.

Newham Council's workplace scheme brings together the needs of both employer and jobseekers. More than 5,000 people have been placed into jobs over each of the last two years, with retention rates at 86 per cent compared to the Department for Work and Pensions' 52 per cent benchmark.

Increasing safety and reducing crime.

Manchester City Council have helped bring about a significant fall in youth crime through a redesign of the criminal justice system. Targeted approaches to reducing reoffending have more than halved repeat offending among eighteen- to 24-year-olds within twelve months of intervention. Some of the most serious offences have fallen by 80 per cent.

Helping families who need it most to overcome their challenges for good.

Oldham's pilot Family Focus Programme has reduced police callouts, A&E attendance and many families' need for mental health and rehabilitation services. This has saved up to £1.1 million and delivered a better service.

Giving every child a good start in life.

Nottingham's Early Intervention City Approach has boosted Foundation Stage school results to above the national average, helped to reduce crime of all types from 53,883 offences in 2008 to 30,403 in 2012. It has also helped to reduce rates of teenage pregnancy among fifteen- to nineteen-year-olds by more than 40 per cent.

These five pledges would give councils the freedom to build upon the brilliant work illustrated by these examples. If councils are able to achieve outcomes such as this without significant devolution from the centre then it shows there is real potential to achieve even more if government properly engages in a localist agenda.

Potentially, local authorities would have access to billions of pounds of current expenditure, bringing decision-making closer to those affected by it and improving outcomes for everyone.

Such an approach would not only devolve decision-making on issues which directly affect people's lives, it would also make meeting the challenge of austerity a more realistic proposition, even in the most deprived communities.

Sharon Taylor, Leader of Stevenage Council and co-chair of Labour's Local Government Innovation Taskforce:

'Labour's radical approach to localism is based on the strong ideals of our movement: democracy, devolution, engagement and individual responsibility. It has three core principles at its heart: people power, collaboration and prevention.

This localism will enable better tailoring of solutions to local need. In Stevenage, for instance, we have pioneered our own 'No More' alcohol project to tackle a growing street drinking problem, where a small number of people were disrupting our community. We worked one-to-one with those individuals and brought local support agencies together. This delivered outstanding outcomes, reduced anti-social behaviour and saved money.

These results cannot be effectively achieved by centralised services designed and delivered from Whitehall. It's not affordable either. We need people to get involved in designing the services they use and take responsibility for outcomes. That is why Labour is pledging redistribution of power and resources to localities, a radical localism. This is our greatest hope of advancing social justice in what will be a challenging decade.'

Catherine West, former Leader of Islington Council and prospective parliamentary candidate for Hornsey & Wood Green:

'One of the proudest days of my life was when the cleaners at Islington Council were paid a living wage. This was what it meant to lead a Labour council, where our values of equality and fairness could make a difference – even in a time of austerity.

It came about because of the Fairness Commission we set up when Labour re-took control of the Town Hall in 2010 – a dialogue between the community, local businesses and leaders in the public sector.

The commission paved the way for a fairer Islington, recommending a feasible but radical approach: the living wage; universal free school dinners for primary school children; 2,000 genuinely affordable homes by 2015; local educational and employment opportunities for young people – all delivered despite drastic cuts to local government funding.

We can restore faith in politics by fighting for the things that matter. I joined the Labour movement to make a difference and give people hope. In Islington, we made a good start.'

Further and faster

Notwithstanding the benefit of the five core pledges, there is the opportunity to achieve even more by going further and faster.

Analysis by Ernst and Young of whole-place community budget pilots suggests even greater integration working on health and social care could save the national exchequer between £5.8 and £12 billion over a five-year period.

Equally, if community-style budgets were introduced to tackle worklessness they estimate benefits of between £3.1 and £5.9 billion over the same period.

We also know that the current prison population of 85,000 (one of the highest in Europe) costs an estimated £3.6 billion per year, with half of crime committed by people who have already been through the criminal justice system. Working locally to reduce reoffending has again shown the opportunity to reduce those costs.

Such savings would not only contribute to the austerity challenge, but a shared reward model would allow reinvestment into key services, which looks impossible under the current centralised system at the current time. All are worthy of consideration.

While the new English deal should be available to all councils, unitaries, counties and districts, the pace of devolution to deliver for communities should move at the speed of the fastest, not the slowest.

Labour's Local Government Innovation Taskforce has therefore recommended a twin-track process that enables some councils to go further and faster as part of the deal. Where local authorities have a strong track record of successful delivery and effective statutory governance arrangements, they should be able to negotiate further devolution of powers and funding.

The taskforce has therefore proposed that in areas where costs and demand are high, pressures are complex demand pressures and public services require reform to better meet these needs, Labour will offer 'deals' between the centre and local authorities on:

- Health and social care intervention
- Tackling worklessness
- Reducing re-offending

It underlines that what Labour has to offer is a more radical and different localist model than anything currently on offer.

Jules Pipe CBE, Mayor of Hackney and co-chair of Labour's Local Government Innovation Taskforce:

'Over a decade, Labour has taken Hackney Council from being the worst local authority in the country to one that innovates and provides local solutions to deliver better results than approaches prescribed by Whitehall.

Examples include: the extremely successful re-engineering of children's social care; growing the borough's economy by playing a crucial role in the development of Tech City; dramatically reducing youth offending and gun and knife crime through the country's first Integrated Gangs Unit that fully co-locates all relevant professionals; and building the highest number of council homes in the country in recent years through innovative cross-subsidy models.

Like many councils across the country we are ready to go further and faster to deliver more for our residents. Only a Labour government committed to localism will enable us to achieve our full potential.'

Delivery and accountability

With power comes responsibility and with that the need for accountability. If ministers are to release the levers of power, devolution needs to be accompanied with a model for good governance and effective checks and balances. Central government will require assurances that services can be delivered to sufficient standard and that local communities have a real voice in activities being delivered on their behalf.

There would also be a need for local oversight and scrutiny. Accountability has to go down as well as up.

Labour would fill this gap by introducing a legal requirement for local authorities to set up a Local Public Accounts Committee (LPAC). Made up from a majority of backbench councillors, a LPAC would have oversight of all public expenditure for the area on behalf of local people and could make recommendations where it saw fit. It would ensure openness, transparency and could also be the 'go-to' body for local people seeking to redress any dissatisfaction.

The impact made by Labour's formidable chair of the House of Commons' own PAC shows the difference this could make in improving accountability. Every town, city and community should have its own Margaret Hodge.

Changing role and behaviours – pushing power beyond the town hall

As alluded to earlier, devolution of decision-making to local councils does not guarantee greater influence to local people if local politicians ignore the opportunity to devolve and engage even further.

Indeed, the need for councils and councillors to behave differently has been accelerated by austerity. Without the resources historically available, local government has to find new ways to solve problems.

There are already good examples in Labour local government where councils are trying to do just that.

Oldham Council's co-operative approach is focussing on what works for different neighbourhoods, and building success on strong relationships between ward members, locally based services and communities. To that end, the council has devolved extensive powers to six district town halls with local budgets and supporting staff. These neighbourhood working arrangements are designed to build local relationships and be about co-operative opportunities for service delivery.

Sunderland Council's Community Leadership Programme has decentralised local public services to five areas within the city, including the governance and delivery of environmental (street scheme) services, youth services and prioritisation of local highways maintenance activity. This has involved budgets of over £15 million being subject to local influence at an area level so that decision-making can be more responsive to local needs. Area-based budgets with a combined value of over £1.5 million enable councillors to work closely with communities to establish local priorities, strengthening engagement and helping manage demand by promoting self-help.

Durham County Council established fourteen Area Action Partnerships as an engagement mechanism and a means through which to deliver action on locally determined priorities. Over 11,000 people are members of AAP Forums which undertake project work to develop and implement ideas. The council allocated £21 million to deliver local priorities (which has brought in a further £34 million match funding) and through participatory budgeting exercises people have been able to vote for local projects. Almost 19,000 people have voted in participatory budgeting events allocating over £1.5 million to 300 projects.

Devolution from the centre will require such approaches to become the norm if the objectives of better outcomes at less cost are to be achieved. This is, however, a difficult process. Councils, staff and councillors will require a new set of skills, aptitudes and approaches. Community governance looks very different from most corporate governance models, which have hitherto been the norm.

We need development programmes for officers and members alike to help make this transition a reality. Labour's Local Government

Innovation Taskforce has suggested a college of local representation as a potential solution.

Acting local

An incoming Labour government will find itself in the most difficult position of any new Labour administration since the Second World War. Rather than seeing local democracy wither on the vine, there is an opportunity under Labour to revitalise its role.

A 'localism' strategy built on good evidence already on the ground with strong accountability would help transform people's lives and build a better Britain – a real alternative to David Cameron and Eric Pickles's policies of managed decline.

As experience in many Labour councils already shows, progress can be achieved when money is tight, but only if politicians at all levels are prepared to let go of the levers of power and, above all, trust the people they serve. Done right, real local devolution can not only improve outcomes and save money, but also help restore public faith in our democratic institutions.

In short, Labour will think national but act local. It is only by voting Labour that we can reinvigorate our public services, re-establish strong, local democracy and strengthen our communities. If you want a greater say over what happens in your area and for politics to be more responsive to the issues where you live, then vote Labour.

Sir Steve Houghton CBE is the Leader of Barnsley Metropolitan Borough Council and a member of Labour's Local Government Innovation Taskforce.

Chapter 11

Britain in a Complex World

DOUGLAS ALEXANDER MP

'Our foreign affairs are, of course, our most important public affairs.'
— Adlai Stevenson, American statesman and ambassador to the United Nations, 1961–5

The foreign policy challenges that the UK faces in the middle of this decade are very different to the ones we faced in the middle of the last.

Labour knows that the world around us is changing and that the two pillars on which our foreign policy has for decades been based – the transatlantic relationship and our membership of the European Union (EU) – are both today being challenged by new developments in the geo-political environment.

After more than a decade of war abroad and amid budget cuts and political gridlock at home, our most important ally, the United States, is stepping back from its decades' long role as the world's police officer. It is also rebalancing its priorities to Asia and the Pacific while reducing its level of engagement in Europe. Europe itself is gripped by an economic and social crisis on a scale not seen since the '30s.

At the same time, the destiny of the Middle East hangs in the balance as violence and volatility, more than nascent democracy, marks the wave of change still sweeping that region. A global shift of economic power from west to east is underway, accelerated by the severe impact of the 2008 financial crisis on the West.

And yet, what is striking about much of the debate on foreign policy within the present government, is just how limited it is – often dominated by three themes: the latest crisis in the news; intermittent concern for the state of our 'special relationship' with the United States; and, most persistently, indeed incessantly in David Cameron's case, our relationship with the EU.

Unlike this current government, Labour has not, and will not, shy away from engaging with some of the tough questions that the next government will inevitably have to face in foreign policy.

Among them, how do we ensure an equilibrium between our ambitions and our capability in foreign policy? How do we respond to the challenge and opportunity of the rising powers? How do we focus less on debating the 'specialness' and more on building the 'relationship' we have with the United States? How do we best protect ourselves and keep our citizens safe in an insecure world? And how should we orient ourselves to what looks like epoch-making change underway in Asia?

In addition, through engaging and answering some of these key questions, Labour will not just change the government, we will also work to change our country – and with that, our country's place in the world.

Vernon Coaker MP, shadow Secretary of State for Defence:

'After the end of combat missions in Iraq and Afghanistan, the time is now right to consider what role we want our armed forces to play in the world. The ever-changing and unpredictable nature of global security challenges means that Britain's role is a hugely important one.

Labour will make it a priority to ensure that the next Strategic Defence and Security Review and the National Security Strategy provide the long-term direction that UK defence and security requires – one that is fiscally realistic and strategically ambitious.

We know we must strengthen and deepen our partnerships with existing allies and seek to cultivate new ones if we are to achieve our strategic objectives. UK defence is at a crossroads and the public is ready and willing for wide-ranging and open debate on the way forward. Labour will lead, encourage and shape that debate.'

Sophy Gardner, Labour's prospective parliamentary candidate for Gloucester:
   'I left the RAF with nineteen years' service under my belt and was finally free to get actively involved in politics and with the Labour Party. The party shares my values and those of many of us in the military: working together, and the importance and value of every member of your team.

So many people's lives have been touched by the armed forces, as I've found in Gloucester. As we enter a debate about what role our servicemen and women will play in the future, I know Labour really is the party of defence and the armed forces.'

An Asian step change

Today, as economic wealth and political power shifts from west to east, the UK is lagging behind many European partners in its quest to gain from Asian growth markets and to build political relationships with rising powers. A Labour government would re-orientate its strategic focus to meet the challenges and opportunities of Asian revival. Too much of the current government's shift to Asia has been narrowly focused in the commercial realm, but the evidence suggests that even if the UK's prime interest were mercantile, it would be more likely to benefit from economic openings if its growth strategy were anchored in a broader political approach led from the highest levels of the government.

So, the next Labour government will set up an 'Asian step change' taskforce, supported by the Foreign and Commonwealth Office (FCO), to flesh out the strategic goals for government departments in the most economically dynamic and geo-politically perilous region of the world.

This could include a foreign and security policy strategy with elements on the key global issues as well as Asian security. An important part of this approach should be an attempt to mobilise all parts of the Foreign Office as well as the Ministry of Defence and the Department for International Development to draw on their distinctive abilities to build relationships with Asian countries.

This would go hand-in-hand with a domestic policy push across government to focus our education, infrastructure, inward investment policies and export promotion policies to allow the UK to benefit from Asian growth.

The Middle East

We are witnessing change on a truly historic scale in the Middle East. The initial optimism of the Arab uprisings has been tempered by the horror in Syria, the tumult in Egypt, the ongoing conflict within Iraq. Today there is deep concern that the century-long ordering of nation states in the region is now threatened by a deepening and dangerous sectarian divide between Sunnis and Shia, brutally exposed by of ISIL's campaign across Syria and Iraq.

Recent events in northern Iraq have demonstrated the fundamental danger of the West not possessing a clear strategic framework for coordinating its engagement with the multiple crises now engulfing the Middle East.

It will be vital that the next UK government help ensure that the scale of the challenges emerging in the Middle East be matched by the scale of strategic thinking in the international community's response.

The UK government and its allies should reach out to those regional players who are ready to partner with the international community to help respond to urgent crises, but also to work together to build a better and more stable future for the citizens of the region.

If we are to help these societies to secure a better future, the EU must continue to provide economic assistance and must also take more radical measures to open up European markets to the region. This would benefit European consumers, cement new friendships and help ensure that the political optimism that does exist in the region isn't met with economic disappointment in the medium term.

We must continue the dialogue with Russia on how to address the challenges facing the Middle East. The disagreements with Moscow over Syria have been profound but on other issues, such as Iran's nuclear programme, we have been able to find diplomatic formulae that enable us to work together. We must understand and appreciate Turkey's emergence as a major player across the region and, where we have common cause, work diplomatically together to help stabilise the situation and promote peace and economic development.

Protecting human rights

The strength of our commitment to universal human rights is a key factor in how the rest of the world judges the UK's place on the world stage. The UK was one of the first signatories to the Universal Declaration of Human Rights and, even at a time when the ascendance of democracy and human rights is being questioned, a Labour government would not only uphold those rights, but be a vocal advocate for all other states in the international system doing the same. This applies as much to our partners or allies in other important economic and security endeavours as it does to states with which we have fewer and less important ties.

Our wider commitment to human rights must extend beyond general support to a clear and unambiguous position with regard to torture, which is not only illegal, but abhorrent. Its use under any circumstances cannot be sanctioned. Where there is evidence that unacceptable practices have occurred, be it in countries that are adversarial to the United Kingdom or even among its allies, those practices must be condemned.

In the 21st-century communications environment, our commitment to human rights and the credibility of our public diplomacy are linked and both require us to show our support for freedom of expression on the internet. Today, freedom of speech means freedom to blog, to tweet and to discuss ideas with people all across the world. We must give vocal support to those whose rights are being threatened or removed and support the creation and distribution of technologies that help circumvent illegitimate censorship. This means looking afresh at export control regimes with regard to technologies that may be used for these ends and for the abuse of basic human rights.

And it means supporting the multilateral institutions that include governments and commercial and civil society organisations in the administration of the physical infrastructure of the internet.

Sir Keir Starmer QC, former Director of Public Prosecutions:

'Britain has a proud history on human rights and of standing up for countries across the world who don't enjoy the same freedoms that we can easily take for granted at home. There is a real risk however of this record being undermined by the Tories.

William Hague promised when he was Foreign Secretary that there would "be no downgrading of human rights under this government", but now the Tories are flirting with scrapping the Human Rights Act and withdrawing from the European Convention on Human Rights. This would make Britain the only European country other than Belarus – widely viewed as the Continent's last dictatorship – to be outside the convention and have major implications for our country's standing in the world.

> Human rights are at the heart of everything that Labour stands for: dignity, equality and justice. A vote for Labour is a vote for protecting individual rights against abuses by the state, rather than the Tories' ill-judged rush into isolationism.'

Tackling the threat of climate change

Climate change threatens our economic security. It is a real and present danger to our communities and way of life.

That is why Labour in government will be clear in our commitment to pursue a global multilateral deal to cut carbon emissions and head off some of the worst possible consequences of climate change. With 0.7°C of warming already having occurred, and a further 0.6°C bound to occur from emissions already in the atmosphere, it may be too late to avoid exceeding global warming of 2°C since pre-industrial times, a level that is widely accepted as dangerous.

The projected consequences of sea-level rise, droughts, floods, water scarcity and large-scale population displacement are well known. Warming to even higher levels is possible and, without action, certain.

That is why a Labour government will ensure the UK plays a lead role, including via the European Union, in multilateral efforts to ensure an effective and enforceable agreement to cut global carbon emissions is in effect by 2020. The UK should also ensure that the security implications of climate change remain on the agenda of the UN Security Council.

Yet we must also be willing to form new alliances. There are already professional international networks and cross-country alliances, and the UK should consider what further role it can play to develop new alliances and new instruments to achieve progress. Nonetheless, for many of the poorest countries, climate change is no longer a future threat but already a contemporary crisis. So any development assistance must continue to be targeted and effectively focused on the related challenges of poverty reduction.

Jonathan Reynolds MP, shadow Minister for Energy & Climate Change:

'Tackling climate change should be an issue of consensus, but the Tory-led government has shown worrying ambivalence towards the scale of the challenge.

Despite David Cameron's promises to lead 'the greenest government ever', on his watch the department responsible for adapting the UK to deal with climate change was led by a known climate sceptic, Owen Paterson, for nearly two years. Eric Pickles has used the planning system to block the development of onshore wind, despite it being the cheapest form of renewable energy. George Osborne has repeatedly stressed the costs of moving to a low-carbon economy, when we should be promoting the opportunities for the UK.

Climate change will be even more prominent in the next parliament, with the world's leaders meeting in Paris in 2015 to agree an international agreement on limiting emissions, the successor to the Kyoto Protocol. Only Labour can deliver what the UK needs – both in terms of securing an ambitious agreement and adopting the measures at home to deliver it.'

International Development

Jim Murphy MP, shadow International Development Secretary:

'For progressives the world over, politics is about change. At home we are about challenging inherited disadvantage and creating a country where working-class parents have middle-class children.

Many people retreat into a sentiment that politics changes nothing, but a generation of progress on aid and development shows the difference a vote for Labour can make across the globe. The last Labour government led the world, brokering global agreements to drop the debt, halving poverty and getting more children into school. The next Labour government can go even further.

We can tackle the real driving force of inequity – a fundamental imbalance of power that leaves far too many unable to live their lives to their potential. Labour will focus on economic power, but social and political power as well.

That's why we will put human rights at the heart of our approach, we will help developing countries improve their tax base, we will act on modern-day slavery, and we will fight to put climate change and universal health coverage at the centre of new global agreements on development.

And we will win the argument that development is also in Britain's best interests. The UK would be immeasurably better off growing and trading within a strong global economy with a sustainable climate, supported governments and secure borders. That's what British development helps to achieve.'

Melanie Ward, Labour and Co-op prospective parliamentary candidate for Glenrothes & Central Fife:

'We're Labour because we believe passionately in social justice. These values don't stop at the UK border, they span the globe. From Bangladesh to Tanzania to the West Bank, I've seen first-hand the very real difference that British aid makes to some of the poorest and most marginalised people in our world.

I've worked with women from Afghanistan to whom British aid means the ability to stand up and take action against the horrific violence that so many of them face. I've worked with Kenyan farmers who need the support provided by great British charities just to survive, as climate change turns their land to dust. And I've worked with activists from across Africa on campaigns against tax-dodging because it robs poor countries of the funds to build schools and hospitals. All of these people – and all of us – need a progressive Labour government to once again lead the world in fighting poverty.'

Reform in Europe, not exit from reform

This country is not alone in seeing the public mood towards Europe change in recent years. Despite the global economic trends that have acutely affected countries across the continent, politicians in Europe have faced growing scepticism from their citizens about the case for the EU in the twenty-first century.

EU leaders now bear a heavy responsibility to show that they are willing to learn the lessons of the past and most importantly, learn the right lessons for how to move forward. In particular, that means engaging with the scale of the challenge that they individually and collectively have to face.

If we allow the strains within the EU to turn into open division, the UK will see its own power diffused and its prosperity diminished. Our membership of the EU gives us access to, and influence in, the biggest global trading bloc as well as real opportunities to secure new markets across the world for our products. So, Labour government will be as bold in defending membership of the EU as we are in pushing for real change in Europe.

First, our reforms will help deliver a Europe focused on jobs and growth. An EU Commissioner focused on growth and an independent audit of the impact of any new piece of EU legislation on growth would be key to helping re-focus the Union on this key task.

Second, Labour's reforms will help ensure that EU citizens seeking work here are expected to contribute to our economy and to our society. So Labour will extend the period of time that people from new member states have to wait before being able to come to the UK to look for work. Labour will work to stop the payment of benefits to those not resident in this country and have called on the government to double the time that an EU migrant has to wait before being able to claim the basic Jobseeker's Allowance.

Glenis Willmott MEP, Leader of the European Parliamentary Labour Party:

'Our EU membership is crucial for British jobs and our economy. We need a strong voice to make sure the EU works best for Britain. Labour's work in European Parliament shows we are a party who can make a difference for British people through the EU.

Labour MEPs have backed new laws to curb bankers' bonuses and restrict the casino culture in the finance sector, backed reform of the EU budget, and pushed for a renewed focus on jobs and growth, such as our campaign for programmes to help young unemployed people into work or training. We've fought hard in the European Parliament for clear food labelling and stood up to the tobacco companies with a ban on products that encourage children to smoke. We have acted to end rip-off mobile phone roaming charges, and fought for more rights for air passengers.'

Any agenda for change in Europe must also address people's concerns about how power is exercised at a European level. Labour does not support a drive towards an 'ever-closer union'. Labour has called for national parliaments to have a greater role in EU decision-making by being able to 'red-card' any new EU legislation before it comes into force.

No one is today calling for more powers to be transferred from Britain to Brussels. However, given the uncertainty about precisely what a changing Europe and further integration in the eurozone might involve, Ed Miliband has acknowledged that a further transfer of powers remains unlikely, but possible. That is why a Labour government will legislate for a new lock: there would be no transfer of powers from the UK to the EU without an in/out referendum.

So, the choice in 2015 is between a Conservative Party that

continues to unravel over Europe and a Labour Party committed to working to make the EU work better for Britain.

Foreign policy begins at home

A key challenge for UK foreign policy is to keep pace with the present rate of change in international affairs and global politics. That is why Labour has said that a new government coming to power in 2015 should conduct a Strategic Diplomacy Review. This should assess diplomatic priorities and the relative distribution of expenditure in relation to those priorities, including an assessment of expenditure on conflict prevention as compared to the costs of conflict and post-conflict reconstruction, and an assessment of expenditure on multilateral activities as compared to bilateral activities and the costs of the embassy network. The review would also allow a diplomatic service skills assessment to be undertaken.

Vital economic renewal at home will not only improve the lives of our citizens but will also provide the resources we need to engage successfully in the world for the long term. Indeed, if we can re-create an economic and social model that others want to emulate, it will strengthen our 'soft power' abroad.

So, Labour is clear that if the UK approaches the challenge of the future by acknowledging the ways in which foreign and domestic policy can support each other in this way, then there is no reason why the country cannot continue to be effective and influential on the international stage for many years come.

Conclusion: foreign policy at the crossroads

Modern Britain exists in a world of quite extraordinary interdependence, and the fundamental weakness with this Conservative government's foreign policy is that they remain damagingly unreconciled to that defining truth of our modern age.

Labour knows that for Britain to now try and retreat from the world would be as foolish as it would be futile. The security and prosperity of each and every citizen of Britain now depends on the security and well-being of those who live far beyond our shores.

So today British foreign policy stands at a crossroads.

And a Labour government in 2015 must, and will, be ready to face up to the profound challenge of how to re-think our way to a UK foreign policy agenda that protects our own interests, promotes our values and effectively responds to the changing challenges of our times.

As we approach the next general election, the Labour party will continue to make the case that it is a Labour government, driven by progressive values and a clear sense of the national interest, that will be best able to respond to those new and emerging challenges in 2015.

Douglas Alexander is the Member of Parliament for Paisley & Renfrewshire South and the shadow Foreign Secretary.

Conclusion

DAN JARVIS MP

Before the 1945 general election, George Orwell wrote of a Britain buffeted by the forces of change and a society craving a better future. He told of a generation preparing to place their hopes in Labour, and of people from all backgrounds and occupations who would go on to cast their vote for Clement Attlee's party at the ballot box. Orwell described them as 'the people who feel at home in the radio and ferro-concrete age'.[36] Seventy years on, the general election of 2015 will be won by the party that this generation trusts to meet the challenges of a new and very different age – an age of Twitter, Sky+ and Google Glass.

It is an age of great dangers, demands and difficulties, but also immense promise and potential.

When I think about the task facing my generation of politicians in navigating it, I think of my three young children. They are my priority and shape my politics. Their generation could feasibly live to see the twenty-second century. Like every parent I want their only limit in life to be the reach of their ambition. I think what sort of world they will live in, and ask what can we do now to create a better life for them in twenty or thirty years' time?

This book has sought to show how a Labour government would start that work so that we and future generations can live in a more powerful Britain.

---

36   George Orwell, *The Lion and the Unicorn*, 1941.

It is a vision for a future where we each have more money in our pockets, greater protection from forces beyond our control and greater means to each make a better life for ourselves.

Because far from feeling at home in this rapidly changing world, too many people feel lost in it. I've seen it too often in the people I've met over the past few years.

They include parents like Sally, who has worked all her life. Now she only avoids having to choose between heating and eating by relying on vouchers from the local food bank because her money won't stretch to cover her gas and electric bills.

They include small business owners like Jack, who came to see me with his metal work company on the brink of closure because he was still awaiting late payments from companies owing him thousands of pounds. Despite having a full order book for the next six months, no bank would lend him the money he needed to tide him over and avoid bankruptcy.

And they include women like Jane, who gave up her job to look after her elderly father Andrew. She was frustrated that the system wasn't giving him the stimulating care he needed for his dementia, and felt forced to take matters into her own hands.

Like many people, Sally, Jack and Jane felt like Britain wasn't working for them anymore. Their lived experience shows why Labour's opponents at the next election will not solely be David Cameron and Nick Clegg.

Our adversary is the powerlessness that their inaction and misguided policies have failed to address, and that holds us back in the effort to achieve a fairer, more just and more powerful Britain.

The stakes for the coming general election could not be higher. The British people will have a clear choice.

More of the same under a complacent Tory government content to sit back and let the market dictate the shape of our future, or a Labour government with the energy and ideas to put power, wealth and opportunity into the hands of the many.

The chapters of this book have expressed how we would work to put this into practice, with each author setting out some of the steps that a Labour government would take to create an economy for the many, a more inclusive society and a better politics.

Andrew Adonis, Chuka Umunna and Rachel Reeves described how our vision for Britain's success is founded on a plan to build an economy ready for the future.

The key question that all parties will need to answer at this general election will not be whether people are better off since David Cameron became Prime Minister. Forecasts have already shown that the answer to that question will be no.

The urgent question will therefore be how we upgrade our old economy to a new economy to ensure that the people of Britain are better off in the next five years and the decades beyond.

Labour's answer to that question is the 'high-productivity, high-skilled and innovation-led economy' that Chuka Umunna set out; an economy that creates more good middle-income jobs, spreads opportunity across the whole United Kingdom, and generates the sustainable growth we need to reduce the deficit caused by the global financial crisis.

Ours will be a 'smarter and more entrepreneurial' government, as Andrew Adonis described. We will extend prosperity to all parts of our country by giving our towns and cities the powers, tools and resources needed to get our regional economies firing on all cylinders.

Labour will also back our nation's wealth creators. I want the next Bill Gates to come from Barnsley, Brighton or Bristol rather than Beijing, Baltimore or Bangalore.

Our government will take action to give businesses the support they need to become the success stories of the future: a proper British investment bank, a Small Business Administration and cutting business rates for 1.5 million firms.

And where we find broken markets that 'weaken our society' and 'put limits on our nation's economic success' – as Chuka described

– we'll fix them. That commitment starts with Ed Miliband's plan to reset our energy market and increase competition in our banking sector so that they work better for consumers and businesses alike.

So a vote for Labour is a vote that will empower the employees who work the shifts as well as the employers who create the jobs.

Rachel Reeves reminded us in her chapter how our party was founded on a belief in the value of work. That belief still endures today, but too many people across our country are struggling to keep their heads above water even after a hard-earned pay packet.

As Rachel said: 'We cannot succeed as a country if all the gains of economic growth are concentrated in the hands of a privileged few while increasing numbers of people feel they are working harder, for longer, for less.'

A vote for Labour is a vote for an economy that works for the many, not just the few at the top. It is a vote for dignity in work, with a decent wage that you can live on, a minimum wage that will rise by more than average earnings in the next parliament, and an end to practices like the exploitation of zero-hour contracts that promote powerlessness in the workplace.

We will also give parents the power to continue to work after starting a family, expanding free childcare to twenty-five hours a week for three- and four-year-old children. As Lucy Powell said in her chapter, 'this will give parents trying to juggle working life with childcare outside of school hours the reassurance they need' and make life just that little bit easier for mums and dads across the country.

These are Labour priorities because we know it doesn't just make sense for our economy, it makes sense for our society.

We all lead happier and more fulfilling lives when we have time we can spend with our friends, money left over at the end of the month to treat our loves ones, and stability to save for a rainy day.

For many families that stability starts with a roof over their head and a community where they can put roots down for the future.

I remember how much of a difference it made to mine when I was able to scrape the money together for my first home at the age of twenty-seven. Today, record numbers of young adults are living with their parents into their early thirties, 1.6 million people are stuck on housing waiting lists and short-term tenancies mean many families who rent are forced to find a new home every year.

A vote for Labour is a vote to close the gap between people's aspirations to own their own home and the likelihood that they ever will. We will build 200,000 houses a year by 2020 and make stable tenancies the norm for people who rent.

A vote for Labour is a vote for giving our young people not only a foot on the housing ladder, but more opportunities and better prospects.

One of my predecessors as a Member of Parliament for Barnsley Central was Roy Mason. Nearly eighty years ago, Roy began his working life down the pit as a miner at the age of fourteen. Elected to Parliament, he rose to serve with distinction in some of the most demanding Cabinet positions during the '70s.

My ambition for Britain's future is a more socially mobile nation, one where the daughter of a cleaner from Kingstone in my constituency has as much chance of serving at our country's top table as the son of a barrister from Kingston-upon-Thames. That's my idea of social justice.

Labour will strive for this by equipping our young people for the careers of tomorrow, as Bex Bailey set out in her chapter.

A vote for Labour is a vote to tackle overcrowded classrooms and make sure every child receives quality teaching relevant to the lives they'll lead in the internet age, including better relationship education.

Our government will ensure that a university degree remains a route but not the only route to a successful career, with better vocational education and more gold-standard apprenticeships. We will tackle the scandal of long-term youth unemployment, guaranteeing a job and training for any young person out of work for more than twelve months.

And we will make sure we leave behind a good legacy for future generations. Labour will be ready to respond to the challenge of climate change where the Tories have dragged their feet, and be a government that will begin reducing the national debt when this government has increased it.

Bex reminded us however that as well as being part of our future, young people also 'have so much to give to the here and now'. That is why our government would give more teenagers a vote in our democracy and a stronger voice in our public services.

A vote for Labour is a vote for reforming our public services so that they are shaped to serve people, rather than people being shaped by public services.

Steve Reed identified in his chapter how 'too many of our existing public services deal with failure rather than preventing failure from happening in the first place'. A Labour government will work to change this by prioritising prevention. In a time of tight budgets, this is not only the smart way to deliver better outcomes but the best way to ensure value for money.

This principle is especially relevant to the future of our NHS. One only has to look at how diabetes consumes 10 per cent of our health budget each year, or the £13 billion we spend every year on the consequences of mental health conditions largely untreated in childhood.

As Liz Kendall relayed in her chapter: 'Helping people stay healthy and intervening early on to prevent problems getting worse is essential to improving people's quality of life and reducing spending on more expensive hospital and residential care.'

A vote for Labour is a vote for a party you can trust to put this principle into practice, protecting our NHS by reforming it to meet new challenges. We will empower patients by bringing back the guaranteed access to a GP appointment within forty-eight hours that David Cameron took away, and deliver an integrated system of physical, mental and social care that treats patients as whole people rather than individual problems.

And we will extend this people-powered approach to our local public services, ending the Cameron culture of localism on paper and centralism in reality.

It's why a vote for Labour is a vote for stronger communities. By sharing power across the country and shifting decision-making to people on the front line, we will give people the capacity to find local solutions to local problems, from getting people back into work to stopping youth crime before it starts.

We will also offer a progressive approach to issues like immigration that have had the potential to divide some communities in the past. We will listen to people's concerns, tackle unfairness and exploitation, and introduce smarter and more effective controls in the way David Hanson and Polly Billington described.

I've seen in my own community how people engage with politics much more positively when they are invited to be part of a real local decision-making process rather than consenting to choices already made for them. Labour's ambition will be to make this the norm rather than the exception.

As Sir Steve Houghton outlined: 'Done right, real local devolution can not only improve outcomes and save money, but also help restore public faith in our democratic institutions.'

Restoring this faith is essential. The challenges facing Britain today are too great for politicians to tackle alone, distrusted and disconnected from the rest of society.

As Stella Creasy wrote in her chapter: 'It is only when each of us plays a part in addressing them – as citizens, consumers and campaigners – that we can truly overcome them in a way in which all can benefit.'

It's part of how we create a confident country made up of more powerful people, ready to stand tall on the world stage.

I've never believed that politics should stop at the water's edge. Globalisation means closing ourselves off from the world today simply isn't an option.

A vote for Labour is a vote for a government that will work globally as well as locally to create a better life for people at home. As
Douglas Alexander described, we will protect jobs by maintaining our
commitment to membership of the world's largest trading bloc. We
will pivot towards Asia, preparing our country for an era more likely
to be defined by the rise of Beijing than the reach of Brussels. And
we will work together with other countries to keep Britain safe and
tackle the biggest international challenges that we cannot face alone.

Alan Johnson MP, former Home Secretary:

'When Labour came to power in 1997, there were 2.6 million pensioners
living in abject poverty, in the NHS things were so bad that one in every
twenty-six patients on the cardiac waiting list died before they could
be operated on. Crime had doubled under the Tories and educational
attainment, particularly in London, was so bad that only about a third
of students achieved five decent GCSEs.

By the time we left government, all of this had been utterly transformed. There was a minimum wage, a pension protection fund, an
education maintenance allowance and thousands of Sure Start children centres across the country. There had also been five successive
quarters of growth as Alistair Darling brought Britain through the
global financial crisis.

Don't let the Tories and their supporters in the media re-write history.
We were a good government and will be again.'

So, why vote Labour?

I began this book by writing about trust and the sense many people have that our problems have outgrown our politics. I remain
convinced that restoring people's faith in politics will be the
greatest challenge facing my political generation, but I conclude

this book positive that Labour is a party ready to prove equal to the task.

I do not pretend that a Labour government will be able to solve all of our national problems if we win the next election. No government can do everything. Big change takes a national effort, a country working together for the good of all.

It will be hard too. Labour would not be able to reverse all the decisions the Tories have made these past four years, and further tough choices will be necessary. But I can promise you this: Labour will be the party on your side. When difficult decisions need to be made, and this changing world brings new pressures upon our lives, Labour will fight for the many rather than the few. We will be fair government.

We will stand up for all, from the young graduate desperately searching for a job in Dundee, the apprentice looking for a better job in Lincoln, the small business owner looking to expand in Plymouth, the commuter trying to find the money to get to work in Reading, the family struggling to keep with the rent in Croydon, the young couple dreaming of buying a home in Cardiff, the pensioner choosing between heating or eating in Carlisle, the disabled woman paying the Bedroom Tax in Redcar, and the victim of crime in Norwich who needs someone to stand up for her rights. They all know it's time for a change.

David Lloyd George once said – speaking a few months after Britain's first ever Labour government took office – that 'a tired nation is a Tory nation'.[37]

More than three decades later, his words would be borrowed by an American President summoning his country to compete in a changing world where 'the balance of power is shifting' and 'the old ways will not do'.

'This is not a time when the United States can afford to be either tired or Tory,' said President Kennedy.[38] The lesson he drew from

---

37   David Lloyd George, Speech to the London Liberal Federation, 12 May 1924.
38   John F. Kennedy Presidential Library and Museum, Speech to Democratic National Convention, 15 July 1960.

those words for his country half a century ago is the same one for ours today.

This is a moment when we should be unleashing all our collective energies to seize this moment and create a more free, prosperous and powerful Britain.

My hope for 2015 is that when people look back in years to come they say it was when Britain turned the page, struck out anew and became authors of our own destiny once again.

That is the more powerful future that Labour will work for and we invite you to join with us.

Acknowledgments

My life outside of politics taught me the value of teamwork, and this book has been a team effort. I would like to thank everyone who has contributed, from the leader of the Labour Party to all those who provided chapters, quotes, advice and guidance.

I would like to thank Iain Dale and his excellent team at Biteback for their patience and advice, as well as Jason Keen and Paul Richards for their invaluable support. Without them the book would not have happened.

My wife Rachel has also pointed out that there would have been no book without her support! She is right of course and I would like to thank her – not just for the book, but for all the other stuff.

Above all, I would like to thank our members. Those who we sometimes refer to as the 'fighters and the believers'. Those who turn out whatever the weather to knock on doors and deliver the leaflets, and who place their trust in our party to stand up for the many and not just the few. They know that membership of our party is not always a bed of roses. This book is for them.

About the Editor

Dan Jarvis has spent his life working in public service, first in the armed forces and then as a Member of Parliament. In January 2011 he became the first person since World War Two to resign his commission in order to contest a parliamentary by-election.

Originally from Nottingham, he graduated from Aberystwyth University in 1996 with a degree in International Politics and Strategic Studies before attending the Royal Military Academy Sandhurst.

He was commissioned into the Parachute Regiment and subsequently deployed to Kosovo, Northern Ireland, Sierra Leone, Iraq and Afghanistan.

During his service his postings included: Platoon Commander in 1 Para, Aide de Camp to General Sir Mike Jackson, Adjutant of 3 Para and staff planner in the Permanent Joint Headquarters. He also served as a Company Commander in the Special Forces Support Group.

He was elected as MP for Barnsley Central on 3 March 2011 and subsequently awarded the MBE for his service in the army, making him the first serving MP to be decorated for military service for many years.

Dan has served as shadow Minister for the Department of Culture, Media and Sport and, in October 2013, was appointed as shadow Minister for Justice with responsibility for Youth Justice and Victims. He is also the Labour Party's lead for the 100th anniversary commemoration of World War One.

In 2013 and 2014 he ran the London Marathon to raise money for Cancer Research UK. He has also previously led mountaineering expeditions in the Himalayas.

He lives in Barnsley with his three children, his wife and their dog.